The Best Is Found In You

Nancy Lazaro

E & D Vision Publishing

Dar es Salaam

E&D Vision Publishing Limited
P.O.Box 4460
Dar es Salaam
Email: info@edvisionpublishing.co.tz
Web: www.edvisionpublishing.co.tz

The Best Is Found In You
© Nancy Lazaro, 2014

ISBN: 978 9987 735 19 8

Layout & Design: SANOL

Dedication

For my mother; Clara whose life, love, prayers and support have made me a woman that I am today.

Introduction

The Best is Found in You aims at building a base for young people in conquering the fears and failures of life. It brings the life of a youth and the reality of the world on the same table. It teaches the youth different values that are important to possess in life as well as reminding the youth that the future is created now. It brings forth the basic foundation for every young person to grow up learning the art of life. It focuses on inspiring a young person for greater success, identifying their values and strengths. It includes self-help articles, poetry and other inspirational articles from the author and influential people across Africa, who believe in their dreams and walk the talk.

I was inspired to write this book after I got done with my first degree and realized there are a lot of opportunities to enhance our personal development and act as a driving force for our success but unfortunately we have a blind eye to these opportunities. A lot of young people are like sleeping giants as they have a lot of potentials in them that are yet to be discovered by themselves. A candle cannot bring light unless it is lit up. Young people need to be inspired. Young people are more equipped with hard skills while forgetting soft skills. If we can change the attitudes and perception of young people and make them think positive and work towards the betterment of their societies, then we have achieved more than we can ever imagine. This book is here to inform and inspire. It consists of five chapters as follow;

Chapter 1: Personal Strengths, Weaknesses, Opportunities and Threats (SWOT) Analysis

Chapter 2: Success

Chapter 3: Leadership

Chapter 4: Growth

Chapter 5: Maturity and a world beyond words

The book represents a journey that unfolds as the reader move from one chapter to the other. Chapter one talks about personal strengths and weaknesses that each individual has to realize as well as opportunities and threats that surround them. This helps in personal development and gives direction to a person towards a brighter future. Chapter two discusses successes and the right path that an individual has to take in order to succeed. It explains the principles of success and entrepreneurship as the building block of success. Also the chapter explains on legacy and change as being inspired by success. Good leadership will eventually bring success and one should allow growth to take place within them in order to reach out to greater heights and make a difference in their societies and the world at large. This is explained in chapter three and four. Chapter five includes a collection of poems that are inspiring and focusing on maturity of an individual as well as thoughts of people from different walks of life that are focused on personal development, leadership, developing talents, living your dreams and positive thinking towards life are included.

I hope the book will inspire you and one of the sources of growth and maturity in your life.

Acknowledgement

I do thank God for breathing air into my soul and giving me strength and knowledge to write this book. Special thanks therefore, goes to God Almighty, the Most High, for without him, I am nothing.

I thank my mother for her endless prayers; love and support in writing and making this book a success. Furthermore I extend my gratitude to my brothers, sisters, son and all my family members.

I believe stars are holes in heaven for our loved ones to see us through. Special thanks to my late father, Duncan and my beloved late sister, Wendy, for the love they wrapped me with while they were on earth. Love was born to spread to generations.

There are a lot of people who have helped me in one way or the other in making this book a success and for believing in me and my dreams even when no one saw the potential in them.

God Bless You All.

Nancy.

Table of Content

Chapter 1:

Personal Strengths, Weaknesses, Opportunities and Threats (SWOT) Analysis

Success comes with hard work and commitment to the effective and efficient use of ones gifts and talents. Back in 2008, I was in a National Leadership Development Seminar at Bagamoyo, about seventy kilometers from Dar es Salaam. The seminar was organized by AIESEC, a students' platform for discovering and developing potentials. The conference involved the youth from East Africa who were very active and ready to learn and network. One of the facilitators of the conference put a light in our lives on the personal SWOT analysis and that inspired me to share with you what it is.

SWOT is an acronym for Strength, Weakness, Opportunities and Threats. Strength and Weakness represent the internal characters that one has control over and Threats and Opportunities represent the external characters that a person has no control over.

I had a very hard time writing down my strengths and realizing my weaknesses, threats and opportunities that are around my environment. I have never had a moment in life to analyze myself and know all the strengths that I possess and the weaknesses that I should shy away from. This particular moment was the first time and it was surely a turning point and a solid foundation for my personal success.

Personal SWOT analysis is essential for every individual in order to understand ourselves better and capitalize on our potentials. SWOT analysis helps us to reflect on the positive factors that contribute to the success of an individual as well as the negative factors that are the stumbling blocks to success. It is a tool for personal development including self-awareness, positive thinking towards life, self-knowledge, developing talents and identifying and improving ones potential. SWOT analysis clears your path and gives you a direction towards a brighter future.

There is a deeper understanding of ones' self once a person performs the analysis which can be undertaken by anyone who has hunger for success and personal development. You do not have to acquire certain skills in order to perform a SWOT analysis; you just have to be honesty with yourself in identifying your own strengths and weaknesses that will lead you to exploring the opportunities and undermining threats that you are facing.

Strength

Strengths are distinctive characteristics that a person has which enable him/her to accomplish different tasks. These are the qualities and capabilities that a person possess which may include higher level of self-awareness, self-confidence, self believe, good communication skills, efficient and effective project management, good sense of humor, self-control, good leadership skills, team play character, well equipped interpersonal skills, emotional intelligence and many others.

Knowing yourself involves understanding your capabilities and realizing unique characters you possess that can help in the identification and improvement of your potential as well as progressing in your own personal development. Your strength will help you in building a solid ground for your own good as a person and your career at large. Your personal life success starts with recognizing your strength.

When you think of your strengths, think of the abilities that you possess that are positive, rare, unique or add value to the society. For instance, if you live in a society where 90% of people are active learners then that will not be your strength rather a habit that is integrated in your society.

In order for you to understand your strength, there are several questions that you need to ask yourself and be extremely honest in answering them. These questions are:

- What do you perceive as your strength?
- What skills do you possess over others?
- Do you have connections with decision makers in your society?
- Are you a people's magnet?
- What are the personal resources that you can have easy access to?
- What unique character do you possess over others?
- What do people around you see as your strength?
- What do you do better than anyone else?
- What personal success makes you a proud human being?
- In what areas do you excel?
- Do you have the capabilities, talents and skills in that particular area? Which area?
- Do you have any professional knowledge in that area?

If you have difficulty answering the questions, you can write down your personal characteristics and evaluate your strengths from them.

Ask yourself these questions over and over again, every after a certain period of time. We need to re-do the exercise after a certain period of time because we learn and grow. Gaining knowledge that advances our lives is an ongoing process. Your strength may be advancing every after sometime if you work hard to achieve your potential. Knowing your strength is one thing but using your strength to capitalize on your potential and take advantage of the opportunities in your surrounding is another thing.

Weakness

Weaknesses are the qualities that hinder our personal development thus they are obstacles that inhibits us from achieving our full potential and accomplishing our lifetime goals. These include all characters that do not reach a quality standard that we aspire them to reach, for instance, lack of confidence, disorganized behaviour, poor decision making and poor communication skills.

There are a lot of people who have failed to choose career that suits them well because she/he has never taken time to know her/his weaknesses. Thus she/he chooses any career that she/he desire. She/he let their desire to lead her/him and take control forgetting that fulfilling that desire requires overcoming of personal weaknesses that can frustrate the career and focusing on the strengths which can lead the career to reach its desired peak.

Weaknesses affect negatively personal development and growth therefore becomes an enemy to personal success. In order for a person to succeed, they must make sure that they have full understanding of their own weaknesses so as to conquer them and emerge a winner.

Weaknesses are internal factors and can be controlled. A person whose weakness is lack of self-confidence in speaking to the public can only eliminate the weakness through constant practice of speaking to oneself in front of the mirror thereafter, progressing to smaller audiences and eventually to bigger audiences. The key to minimizing and finally eliminating your weaknesses is to accept that you are weak in a certain area and then to work towards turning your weaknesses to strengths thus completely eradicating them.

The following questions will guide you in the process of identifying your weaknesses so as to eliminate them from your life and walk along a path of success;

- What do you perceive to be your weaknesses?
- What do people around you see as your weakness?
- What are the activities that you always avoid to do because you don't feel comfortable and confident doing them?
- What are the negative life practices that you possess?
- What do you fear the most as you pursue your career?
- What are your main limitations in this area?
- What skills and abilities are needed to defeat the weakness in you?
- Which area in life do you think people need to improve?

Thus, not knowing ones weaknesses can simply lead to destroying oneself through choosing a wrong career, performing poorly in respective fields, being ignorant about the threats around you and not being able to prepare yourself to succumb to these threats. Knowing your weakness is an important step for personal growth and development.

Opportunities

Opportunity is an opening, a chance, a situation or a possibility for a person to be able to do something in a certain environment. Usually, opportunities are the external factors that enhance one's personal development thus helping them achieve their desired goals. You have to make use of any opportunity that may support you in reaching out to your dreams.

Opportunities are many. Take a look around you, think of the world that surrounds you. Don't you see anything that you can take advantage of? Is there anything wrong in your community and that people are blaming each other? Are there opportunities in the education sector that can help you advance your career? Is there a new technology that your community has not grabbed yet? Is there anything you can do in the community and benefit from it? Opportunities are everywhere in the world, from where you stand to where you have never been. Print, broadcast and online media has been a great source of information on different opportunities that surround us.

Grasping opportunities will help you to develop as a person and in your career as well as to serve the community around you. For instance, a recently college graduate may recognize an opportunity in organizations that have graduate trainee program which will help them in gaining work experience and knowledge in a certain field. The following questions will guide you in realizing opportunities that are available and are waiting for you to take action:

- What positive change can be made in your life?
- What opportunities do you see that are accessible to you?
- What positive change can be made in your community?
- What would you want to see happening in your community?
- What trend do you foresee in your community?
- What have you encountered recently that may be the opportunity to do something in your community?
- What legacy would you want to leave with your family, community, country and the world at large? You have to be a goal getter. Grab every opportunity that comes your way as long as it is valid, beneficial and can add value in your

life. In short, be opportunistic. There are different levels of risks associated with opportunities therefore, you have to be able to take calculated risks.

Threats

Threats are all factors which may hinder ones' personal growth and development. Threats are a result of external environment and they are uncontrollable. For a recent graduate, threat may be that the job market is saturated making it hard for him to be employed.

I look at myself as a young person and there are threats that are waiting for me to make a wrong move so that they swallow me up. I have seen lives of many young women and men perish as a result of the HIV/AIDS pandemic. This disease is a great threat in the life of a young person as it can take away ones' hope for living and can lead to destroying one's path to a successful career.

I have seen young boys and girls who are involved in drug abuse not knowing that it is one of the great threats to their personal growth and development; health wise, career wise and their lives in general.

School can sometimes be boring. It is the goal that we have set for ourselves to achieve that keeps us waking up every day and waiting to learn something from our teachers. For a young person, dropping out of school as a result of peer pressure or any other reason is a threat to his or her life.

There are so many other threats in the life of a young person, all that is needed is the knowledge of these threats which will enable a youth to combat them and live a positive life that assures them of personal growth and development.

The following questions will guide you in identifying threats that surround you;

- What brings you stress and depression?
- What are the obstacles that you face in life?
- What makes you unable to perform well in your endeavors?
- What de-motivates you?

Be sure that you are aware of all the threats that are within and outside your community as long as they may affect your success.

The following is an example of a personal SWOT analysis that was done by a university graduate.

STRENGTH	WEAKNESS
• Time management	• Low self-esteem
• Creative and Innovative	• Lack of work experience
• Active learner	• Disorganized
• Attention to details	• Cannot work under pressure
• Pro-active	• Anti-social

OPPORTUNITIES	THREATS
• Go for internship to gain experience and build network	• World economic depression
• Enrolling for further studies	• Many graduates are unemployed, the job market is saturated
• Join graduate trainee programs to gain experience	• Technology advancement
• Start a company and become an entrepreneur	• Overflow of foreign expatriates in the country
• Use social media to brand myself	• Competition in the area of my specialization is very high

Chapter 2:

Success

"One little step out of your comfort zone can be a giant step toward life's new dimensions, a genuine "No" to the peer pressure can be a thrilling escape from captivity of negativity. It's all true that someone may see in you what you do not see in yourself, but you don't need any certificate of approval from others to determine what is best for you "– Magulya Meja Kapalata

What is success? Do you know that the meaning of success that you have been having may totally be different from others? Everyone sees success differently. Some see success as having a lot of cars, attaining a certain level of education, getting a good husband / wife, living in a posh neighborhood, wearing clothes by top designers, being famous and all kinds of definitions. What is success to you?

I asked different people on the definition of success, and these are the answers I got:

- I define success differently depending on the situation that I am in and satisfaction I get from the things and activities that I go through every day.
- Success is doing something that you love everyday.
- Being better than you were yesterday and that includes loving today and looking forward for a better tomorrow even though it is not promised.
- I have never defined it, I live it.
- Achieving what you desire at the right time and place.
- Success is the result of what you are struggling for.
- I am the definition of success.

The word success is used as many times as the words "Love" and "God".

Many people think success has everything to do with possessions, wealth and fame. Be honest and not modest or shy to answer the following questions that will guide you in knowing your real understanding of success and if it is positive enough to change and inspire lives or it is negative and selfish.

- What is your understanding of success? What is the driving force for the choice of your understanding of success?
- How does the understanding of your success bring value in the society you live in and the world at large?
- Does it include serving other people or is it for the satisfaction of your own desires?
- After reaching the success that you yearn for, what will be your next step?
- Will the understanding of your success leave a legacy? Will it be something that people will remember you by even when you are long gone?

You can define success in your own terms according to the struggles you have been through, life you are living now, people you interact with, knowledge you acquire daily, experience of living or reference to different cultures in the world and desires of your heart.

Success is being a step further from where you had been. Success is being satisfied with your decision, accepting the things that you do not need and focusing on those you do. It is having hope that tomorrow will be better and being patient with the situations in your life.

Richard Branson believes that, "Money is not the definition of success. Get involved in what's interesting in life and do it the best way you can. It may be that money is a by-product of that and you'll be able to use that money for good use."

In 1989, in her speech to the American Women's Economic Development Corporation, Oprah Winfrey listed her ten personal commandments. This list appears in "Oprah Winfrey Speaks: Insight from the World's most influential Voice", by Janet Lowe.

Oprah Winfrey's Ten Commandments for Success

1. Don't live your life to please others.
2. Don't depend on forces outside of yourself to get ahead.
3. Seek harmony and compassion in your business and personal life.
4. Get rid of the backstabbers. Surround yourself only with people who will lift you higher.
5. Be nice.
6. Rid yourself of your addictions-whether they are food, alcohol, drugs or behavior habits.
7. Surround yourself with people who are smarter than you.
8. If money is your motivation, forget it.
9. Never hand over your power to someone else.
10. Be persistent in pursuing your dreams

Anthony Robbins defined success as "to live your life in a way that causes you to feel a ton of pleasure and very little pain - and because of your lifestyle, to have the people around you feeling a lot more pleasure than they do pain."

Many people want to be successful but they do not walk the talk. Success requires effort, determination and sacrifice. You have to work very hard while maintaining your dignity and integrity in order to be where you aspire to be. To be successful is not as easy as walking at the beach during sunset. It is never an easy road to pass and only those who are committed to their goals will see victory and taste the fruits of their success.

One day, I was thinking about the path that my life has to take. I have had a lot of dreams. I have wanted to achieve and I have had a lot of people who did not believe in my dreams. I have never let anyone stand in my way. Many a time, I have been too broke to do anything but I have always remembered Barack Obama who said "You do not have to be rich to achieve your potentials" and that sentence has worked wonders. I live a life with a purpose and in everything that I do, I want to inspire someone else at the end of the day and be a reason for change in their lives. I have four solid principles that I designed for myself and they do help me daily to stay in the path of achieving my dreams.

1. Dream

A dream is an aspiration, a desire and an imagination to do something or to become someone. It is important to have a dream in life as they give you a direction and a focus to attaining the success that you hope for.

The environments that we are subjected to and the situations that we are exposed to, family, friends, teachers or any other person can influence our dreams so much.

There are short term and long term dreams. For instance, a student's short term dream may be getting a first class degree while their long term goal may be becoming the best gynecologist in the country. Most of the time, the short term dreams should support the long term dreams.

You are more than just a mere human being. You are special and unique, and above all you have a task of turning your dreams to reality and never a nightmare to scare you.

There is no limit to dreaming but you have to know which one of your dreams you will focus on until it is accomplished before you jump into another dream. You may not see the impact of your dream now or you may not witness it being true, but your struggles will inspire generations.

A lot of people give up on their dreams because certain people told them that they cannot do what they want to do and they simply let someone else kill their dreams. If God tells me to let go of my dreams, I will do it because he created me and he has a purpose in my life in this world and I will serve his purpose. No one else has the right and power to destroy your dreams, to tell you that you can't and to choose a destiny for you. If you have a dream, don't allow it to be buried, work on it and let giving up be not an option at all. Do not continue endlessly to light others' dreams while putting yours in darkness. Do not only dream, but dream big.

2. Believe in your Dreams

Do you believe in your dreams? Do you believe in yourself? Do you believe you can do anything? Do you believe in the power of your brain and the power of your mind?

Believing in you is the first step to getting things done. If you don't believe in yourself, which means you are not confident enough to defend your dreams thus no one will believe in you as well.

Believe that you are made special for a purpose and you have to fulfill that purpose. Confidence in yourself is a language on its own that everyone around you will be able to understand if you portray it inside out.

Having confidence and believing in yourself, does not mean that people will stand by your side and support your dreams. There are moments when you will have you and only you to lean on and support yourself. Many people will think you are on the wrong road and they will actually feel sorry for you. If you believe in yourself and your dreams, and that you are doing the right thing at the right time, then no amount of words should ever de-motivate you from going for greater heights.

3. Achieve your Dreams

Believing in yourself without working hard to reach out to your objectives and achieve your goals will mean nothing at all. The sweetest part about studying is understanding what you have read and passing your exams and the sweetest part about struggling and striving for success is accomplishing a goal. Have strategies to direct yourself towards your achievements and always make strategic decisions while taking calculated risks.

The question many people have asked themselves shortly after conceiving a dream is "How do I achieve my dream?"

Dreams can be achieved through hard work, commitment, dedication and focus.

Most of the time, the road to achieving your dreams will be very hard to travel on as it will be filled with a lot of challenges and obstacles but remember, whatever you think of will become. If you choose to fill your brain with negative thoughts then you will not progress to the level that you aspire to be. If you fill your brain with positive thoughts then be sure of reaching your destined destination.

We all have dreams, they may not be the same, but the path to achieving our dreams is similar as it needs full commitment, focus and dedication. All the plans you have and the strategies you have set for yourself have to be implemented in order to achieve your dreams.

4. Inspire

To inspire others is to influence. To inspire is to effect positively, to change a person into becoming a better version of him/herself through going after his/her dreams. Furthermore, it is to bring about to a person a beneficial effect, a desire and confidence to go after what they want.

Every minute there is a new born baby somewhere. The earth is being filled with people who through inspiring each other the world can become a better place. In order to inspire someone positively, you have to lead a positive life. Human beings are mostly inspired by success. When one sees a successful person in a certain field, they get inspired instantly. People want to see success in their lives so seeing it in someone else' life inspires them to believe in their dreams and keep on walking in the path of achieving their dreams.

Doctors have inspired a lot of young people who had dreams of becoming doctors to become one. Successful musicians have inspired many who had a dream of becoming musicians to live fully to their dreams. Activists with a vision to make a difference in the lives of children have inspired others who have passion in taking care of less fortunate children to take action.

There are a lot of people in the society that we belong to who have dreams but they do not have the courage to believe in their dreams and take action in order to accomplish their dreams. If you believe in your dreams and you take time to work on it daily until you accomplish it fully then you will definitely inspire someone else to do the same. In order to achieve your dreams, you must set short term goals and strategies to achieve those goals. For instance, a person who wants to be a professional footballer apart from having a talent, they must dedicate their time to constant and perfect exercises, learning the disciplines of football. They must have the passion and desire for the game. Usually character in and outside of the field will play a great role in one's becoming a pro soccer player. Discipline and hard work are always the keys to success, while practicing hard but smart is important in attaining the needed stamina, One also needs to have a good understanding of the game and skills, all these come from an endless hard work in practicing and perfecting.

Achieve your life goals in order to inspire generations. Through positive things that you will be doing, a lot of lives may be changed, inspired and motivated. We want to achieve our dreams for the satisfaction of oneself but through achieving our dreams we intend to inspire others to achieve their dreams.

"Do have a tendency of writing your dreams and defined, timed goals plan on how to achieve them but most importantly analyze them every day and see where you could have done better and improve, seek a mentor... no promises that u will never be wrong or hurt but be sure that will make you wiser and stronger. DARE for more, never settle for less this world is your playground and your mind the engineer" - Dorice E. Malle

Principles of Success

"You are a diamond and as expensive and valuable as it is, you have to be able to shine above the rest and know your worth and value."

Principles are rules and philosophies that can guide ones behavior towards achievement of a certain goal in life. I have come up with seven principles of success as a foundation for a concrete pathway leading to success. In following these principles, one may realize that, being successful in any of your endeavors does not happen overnight and it requires growth and maturity of your potentials.

These principles emerge from the acronym DIAMOND which simply stand for Demand, Identity, Attain, Measure, Opportunity, Natural and Dare and they are largely responsible for one's success;

1. Demand

In your life, always demand the best out of you and if you don't, no one else will do it for you. Life is about discoveries and adventures. You have to be able to discover yourself every single day.. People always want the best things in their lives and they forget that the best things come from them and them alone. The best is found in you therefore, search within your soul and demand the best out of it. Do not settle for less, your worth and value is more than what you have settled for. Keep running your race and run for the cause, run to discover your abilities and demand the best out of you. Capitalize on your potentials and use your talents to reach out to your set goals in life.

2. Identity

If at this moment you meet a stranger and she asks you, who are you? Describe yourself for me to get to know you? Will you have a good answer for this question? What is your personality? What is your identity? Do you know who you are? If a group of people were given an assignment to describe you, would they say things like, amazing, down to earth, ambitious, patriotic, humble, has a sense of humor and generous or will they say greedy, selfish and harsh. Who are you?

3. Attention

Pay attention to every detail in life no matter how small it is. Many people miss great opportunities in life just because they did not pay attention when the opportunity was right under their nose. You have to pay attention to details in life through being up to date with current issues; reading different books, newspapers and magazines, journals and exchanging ideas with different people. The details in life that you pay attention to will help you to walk the talk and make good decisions in life because you become informed. Paying attention to details will add a lot to your knowledge.

4. Mileage

Life is a journey and you need to take one step at a time. Do not rush into things that you are not sure of and do not engage yourself in things that you have not researched well about in order to understand their pros and cons. If you are in the middle of difficulties in life, if things do not move according to your plans and if today seem so far away from your goals, relax and encourage yourself that a journey of a thousand miles starts with a single step and yes, take that step and you will be amazed by the distance you can go thereafter. Presidents were once primary school students, chief executive officers were once toddlers and doctors were once babies. Take one step at a time and never give up no matter what.

5. Outreach

Giving is a thousand times better than receiving. The more you give, the more your hands become stretched unto others hence the more you receive. Giving does not necessarily mean giving money. A smile means a lot to a person who has lost hope in living. Reach out to communities and offer help when and where you can. Be a source of inspiration to others, brighten children's faces by your smile, love others just the way they are and do not judge people. Reach out to communities and serve people.

6. Natural

Be original. A lot of people mimic popular figures' lifestyles. They forget that everyone was created unique, that is in his or her own way. You are unique and special and you have all reasons to be proud of who you are. Be proud of yourself, just the way you are. Do not live like someone else because that is wastage of time and resources. Love yourself inside out.

7. Dare

You can be anything that you want to be and you can do anything that you want to do. You simply have to take a step forward and erase all the "I CAN'T" and be part of the family of "I CAN". Work hard to achieve your goals no matter the challenges and obstacles. Dream big and believe in your dreams. Dare to follow your dreams until you see a ray of light. Dare to go beyond the sky and leave a mark. Dare to be great.

You are a DIAMOND. Shine and keep on shining.

Success Gives You Legacy

Legacy is the heritage handed down from one generation to another. It can be of positive or negative influence. Parents, teachers, leaders, public figures and professionals pass on legacy to generations.

The way parents live their lives, control their finances, communicate with their children, maintain relationships with their neighbors and people other than their family members has a profound effect on the children. After growing up, it is more likely for children to live a life that they witnessed their parents living. Thus, parents have the power to leave behind good legacy or bad legacy or both.

An effective leader who observes the principles of good leadership will inspire a generation of leaders to follow work ethics as they lead. A corrupted leader, is more likely to pass on the bad legacy of corruption to a generation of leaders.

Every day when the sun sets, I ask myself, what have I done to add value to the lives and change lives positively and if I am dead and gone today, how many people will remember me apart from my family and close friends Of course, I want to leave a good legacy and that is why I use my talent as a writer to inspire and inform others.

When I think of legacy, I think of Mwl. Julius Kambarage Nyerere. He is not with us physically but he will always be in our lives generation after generation. He is a statesman who changed Tanzania for the better. We remember him for his good leadership and being in the front line fighting for our country's independence.

To leave a good legacy, you must add value in the lives of others or change their lives positively. You can't leave a legacy behind if you live your life only for your personal satisfaction. The way you live your life will influence the behavior of those looking up to you thus, naturally you will pass on a legacy, good or bad, the choice is yours. People are always remembered based on what they did on earth that has changed or affected lives. Michael Jackson is being remembered for his unique style of dancing and his amazing music that lives on even after his death. Mother Teresa is being remembered for her passion and dedication to charity work towards the less fortunate.

If you want to be like one of the world's great people , you have to know the path they traveled on to be where they are or they were and to have their names echoing in the minds of many in different generations.

Success in any area of your life builds legacy but in order for legacy to come to its full existence you need to know who you are, what you can do best and if what you can do adds value, change and inspire lives. Choices are ours to make. Whether we choose to live a life that leads to bad or good legacy, it's all up to everyone of us.

Let us use the opportunities we have to bring out the best out of ourselves. The power is in every one of us to burry good seeds into the ground and harvest a lot. We are too many in this world to have a small harvest. We can do this to achieve to the fullest; we should act and live beyond our dreams.

You are your own motivation. Rise beyond the sky.

"Life is full of opportunities for those of us who are willing to open our eyes and see them, those of us who are willing to dedicate most of our time to do smart work and to heed advise, in order to become successful in life, we need to take risks. Tanzanian children have a great deal of these opportunities too. But above all, life is not about financial successes but about self-satisfaction from doing the things we love most, being calm to nature and respectful to our bodies, being able to touch and improve the lives of others and fulfilling the will of God" - Kasinner Emmanuel

Entrepreneurship: The Building Block of Success

An entrepreneur is a person who is innovative thus is involved in the creation of new things. Being an entrepreneur does not mean you can succeed overnight but it is surely a building block for one's success. To succeed, you need to be creative, innovative, committed to your goals and vision, passionate about what you do, be able to take calculated risks , self-disciplined, self-starter, determined and be ready to fail but never give up. Through failures, trials and errors, you will learn, grow and finally prosper.

When an individual is an entrepreneur then automatically he/she is practicing entrepreneurship. Entrepreneurship highly involves grabbing opportunities that arise and using them to an advantage.

Entrepreneurs are ambitious and hard-working. They plan and organize their work to encompass the big picture, their vision.

Individuals who are enterprising are more prone to success as they struggle to do things extraordinary to achieve desired goals. There are different kinds of entrepreneurship and some of them are;

- Social entrepreneurship
- Start-up company entrepreneurship
- Intrapreneurship

Social Entrepreneurship

Social entrepreneurs solve social problems in the society through identifying problems and applying their entrepreneurial skills to bring changes. A social entrepreneur is determined, ambitious and innovative in solving social issues and most of the times they do voluntary works which do not involve profit making rather geared toward giving a positive return to the society thus generating social value. The work of a social entrepreneur is focused on the long term and wide-scale social changes rather than short term and small-scale social changes. Social issues include poverty, abortion, unemployment, alcohol and drugs, education, inequality and the likes. Social entrepreneurship solve these social issues through projects, campaigns, movements, festivals and the highly involvement of not for profit organizations.

Intrapreneurship

Intrapreneurship is an act of exercising entrepreneurial abilities while an individual is employed in an organization. An intrapreneur is a self-starter, an innovative and a risk taker. He/she is someone who will always look for new and profitable ways to perform different tasks in an organization, for instance introducing new products to an organization's product line, discovering new markets that are potential for raising company's profit and market shares, innovating new ways of operation in within company and so forth. Intrapreneurs always get ahead of things in an organization as they are creative, ambitious, calculated-risk takers and self-starters. The top managements are always motivated by the intrapreneurial spirit of their workers thus developing more trust in them and allowing them to climb up the management ladder in their respective fields within organizations.

Start-Up Company Entrepreneurship

The common form of entrepreneurship is that one of starting a new business or businesses. There are a lot of entrepreneurs in this field.

Miriam Kilamiani is a business woman in Dar es Salaam. She owns a business by the name, GIFT SKILFUL EDUCATION DEVELOPMENT TRUST LIMITED. She was a teacher at Jangwani Secondary School. She got an idea of starting a school business after seeing no possibility of making a good living out of her employment by then. She decided to start a nursery school and initially she started with only four kids and her sitting room turned to be a classroom. Students studied for free during the first month before they started to pay school fees of Tshs. 5,000/= per month. This situation took almost five months and the number of children increased to twelve. She then decided to turn her bedroom into another classroom. The number of children rose to 24 the same year. With time, the number of children admitted to her school increased and when it was approaching forty, she had to seek for a loan to build classrooms.

She got a loan and built classrooms. With time, she expanded from nursery to primary school and since her dreams were big enough and her limits were beyond the sky, she decided to expand to a secondary school. She currently has a vision to expand her school to a university in the near future.

We look for resources to start our own businesses yet what we are looking for is just beneath our noses. A creative mind will harvest more than that of a person who does not use his creativity. Most of us are creative but we don't feel the urge to use our creativity to step up the ladder. Business opportunities are many; it is up to you to turn an opportunity into a profitable business.

Opportunities are wide spread from the place you are physically present to those places you can only fantasize about. Many people want to start big which means they have forgotten the saying; think big, start small. They want to invest a thousand Tanzanian shillings today and yield a million Tanzanian shillings tomorrow. They lack patience and perseverance. They do not want to live in a real world but a world full of assumptions and thus they barely get ahead in life unless they have inheritance to explore.

If you want to own your own business and be your own boss in the course of life, you have to be able to take calculated risks. It is very OK to be a risk taker but it is only the wise who dare take calculated risks.

I remember when I was at the university taking my first degree, there was this strong lady, twenty three years old who decided to take advantage of the students at the university by researching about their needs and capitalizing on the opportunities found. She saw that there was high demand for cultural stuffs like sandals earrings, and bangles made out local materials and the university did not have a place where such things were sold She started small, and was only selling to close friends. With time, her business started to grow and a lot of other students started buying things from her. She was carrying her business stuffs in her own big handbag and she would be selling after classes, in the buses, on roadsides and in halls of residence. When she was done with her first degree, she started travel abroad to take more merchandise from and to other countries.

She did not start with millions of money; she started small but she was thinking big. Being an entrepreneur does not require a lot of efforts in capitalizing in your potential and merging them with the opportunities around you. It needs a heart which is ready to be persistent on the road of success towards achieving your goals.

There are so many students who see opportunities in the environment that they live in and they decide to capitalize on them. There are students who started selling printed t-shirts which had different messages to cater for the needs of the students. Personally, I was one of them, I made t-shirts with a message in the front reading "I CAN" and on the back reading "BECAUSE I AM TRULY BLESSED" I got enough profit to cover for my expenses at the university.

When I was in my second year at the university, I started selling frames decorated with catchy inspirational messages. These frames were for decorations in houses and offices. I did not get a loss, it was worth doing it. These businesses were a great experience to me and my career.

You have to start investing in yourself now. If you see an opportunity, do not wait for tomorrow because it will never wait for you to be ready. Act on it today, act on it now. After all, there is a saying that tomorrow never comes, so whatever that you have to do, do it now and do it today.

Time elapses in a speed of light. When you have strength to do things for better, do them. Do not wait till you get old only to realize all the opportunities that you had let them pass you by.

Be your own boss. Start climbing the ladder of entrepreneurship right where you are. Start small but think big. Stand up to the challenges in your life; don't let them pull you down. Do not let opportunities pass you by. You are more than what you think you are. Wake up now, stop wasting your time in things that do not matter.

Act now. Act today.

Genuine Success Inspires Change

"To laugh often and much; to win the respect of intelligent people and the affection of children; to earn the appreciation of honest critics and endure the betrayal of false friends; to appreciate beauty; to find the best in others; to leave the world a bit better, whether by healthy child, a garden patch, or a redeemed social condition; to know even one life has breathed easier because you have lived; this is to have succeeded." Ralph Waldo Emerson

Success brings changes to us, our families and our societies through economic development, giving back and inspiring others to reach out to their dreams and work hard to achieve their goals. Success stirs self-development as well as development of our societies, countries and the world at large. Far from being an accolade, success is somewhat a responsibility. Giving back to the community and contributing to the common good is vital in helping those who are less fortunate and in bringing change to the society.

The following is inscribed on the tomb of an Anglican Bishop at Westminster Abbey (1100 AD):

When I was young and free and my imagination had no limits, I dreamed of changing the world:

As I grew older and wiser I discovered the world would not change, so I shortened my sights somewhat and decided to change my country, but it too seemed immovable. As I grew into my twilight years in one last desperate attempt I settled for changing only my family, those closest to me. But alas they would have none of it!

And now I realize as I lie on my deathbed, if I had only changed myself first, then by example I might have changed my family From then, by example, I might have changed my friends.

From their aspirations and encouragement I would have then been able to better my country, and who knows, I might have even changed the world.

We have to embrace change in order to have a better self and a better world. There is positive change and negative change. You only have to be wise in the choices and decisions that you make for they say, there is a thin line between being wise and being foolish.

Change starts where you are; not where you have ever been. Change starts with your heart, mind and soul. Change starts within you. We have been busy pointing fingers at other people, saying that they should have done this and that, yet we have done nothing at all.

We yearn for a better society and a better world, but how do we get these things if we do not change our attitudes and behaviour in order to bring positive change in our societies. I have seen a lot of people who want a clean environment and they are the ones who throw litter five steps away from the dustbin. I have met people who complain daily over their governments yet they never vote during elections. Change starts with you, within you. It is the success you desire that will bring enormous change in the world.

Chapter 3

Leadership

"If your actions create a legacy that inspires others to dream more, learn more, do more and become more, then, you are an excellent leader" – Dolly Parton

I have a best friend who once told me, Nancy, I do not want to be a leader and I do not want anyone to follow me. I was kind enough to ask why? Personally I have always wanted to be a leader and yes, I am a leader, I lead myself and I lead others when I get a chance to. He told me, "I do not want to rely on people because it is very difficult. I do not want to wait for them to deliver, I want to be myself and only myself, no one to lead or follow." I agreed with him that sometimes as a leader, people get on your nerves, but, being a leader requires a lot of sacrifices. It is not only about telling people what to do and wait for them to deliver, it is beyond that.

A leader is an individual who influences him/herself as well as other people in accomplishing of a particular goal whether it is at home, school, work place or in the community in general. We need to change our mentality to adopt the whole concept of leadership. We are the leaders of ourselves, our families and communities, from us; we make the leaders of the world.

The world tries to swallow talents and abilities; only those who struggle to be what they want to be will be puked out and will stand out from the crowd to make a difference. Leaders make a difference. They add value to the family, society, country and the world. A good leader will walk the talk and inspire his followers to be the best they can be. Mwl. Julius K. Nyerere was a good leader for over twenty years in Tanzania promoting peace and harmony.

Are you a leader? Do you aspire to be one? Let us go through characteristics of a good leader. The following, are the personal traits that every leader has to possess, whether you were born a leader or you are a self-made leader.

Confidence

If you are a leader or aspire to be one, you have to be confident in the matters you partake. A leader draws confidence from other people he works with. Confidence that you portray should be a tool for you to gain trust of others. Your team has to be able to trust you. If your team trusts you, they will do just as you instruct them to do.

Commitment

A leader has to be committed to the roles and responsibilities at hand. Commitment and dedication are the keys to success. Excuses are not for achievers. A leader has to part ways with excuses and be committed to complete tasks within the time allocated.

Creativity

A leader has to come up with different ideas to accomplish the task at hand while maintaining the objectives of the project. A good leader should leave room for creativity to his team.

Personal Responsibility

We spend a lot of time planning how we want our things to be done and delivered but sometimes things happen not as we had planned. A leader will always take responsibility for things that have not happened according to plan. A leader will not put the blame unto others but himself.

Humbleness

A leader is not proud, he does not boast himself. A leader is humble enough to be at a level of his team. A leader has a sense of humour. He does not allow the team to work in fear of him only in the line of making things happen in a satisfactory manner on both sides.

Communication Skills

A good leader practices good communication skills. A leader has to be able to maintain a calm situation when things go astray. A leader has to be able to communicate in a peaceful manner to his/her team when there is a misunderstanding or when passing on information.

Vision

Throughout their entire mission leaders have to have a vision. They know where they are going and where they want to be. They know exactly what they want in life. They set a long term ultimate goal to achieve.

Persistence

Sometimes things do not happen at a pace that you want it to happen. There are things that you would like to happen quickly, like getting results of a job done. A good leader is persistent. In the bundle of the keys that A leader holds, patience and perseverance are the master keys and giving up is never an option.

Integrity

A good leader makes wise decisions that are based on honesty and good moral values. An excellent leader will say what they mean and do what they said they would do.

Daring

An efficient leader dares to do things that have never happened or may put him/her at risk of failure. A leader is open to change, makes use of opportunities that others are afraid to explore and takes calculated risks.

Team Work

A good leader will always work hand in hand with his team. He will not act like a boss and instruct people around while sitting and drinking his coffee. A good leader will get dirty in the mud as he work tirelessly with his team.

Source of Inspiration

A good leader has to be a source of inspiration to his team. The whole team has to be inspired and motivated by their leader. A leader has to set a good example to his followers.

Martin Luther King Jr. in a February 1968 sermon said, "We all have the drum major instinct. We all want to be important, to surpass others, to achieve distinction, to lead the parade.... And the great issue of life is to harness the drum major instinct. It is a good instinct if you don't distort it and pervert it. Don't give it up. Keep feeling the need for being important. Keep feeling the need for being first. But I want you to be the first in love. I want you to be the first in moral excellence. I want you to be the first in generosity."

You cannot lead others until you learn to lead yourself. Admire those on top, and work hard to be on top.

Be inspired to inspire.

Chapter 4

Growth

"Everyone wants to live on top of the mountain, but all the happiness and growth occurs while you are climbing it" -Andy Rooney

You Shape Yourself

Each moment spent in this world, gives meaning to your life. The way you live each day, shapes your life. You design yourself to be who you want to be. You choose your life.

Daily as you grow up, you will learn the bitterness and beauty of life and your schedule today is your future tomorrow. The way you walk the walk today will determine your footsteps in the future which is never too far.

Shape yourself to be the best that you can be. Inspire others and live a positive life.

Shape yourself to purity

Shape yourself to achieve your dreams

Shape yourself to conquer all fears

Shape yourself to rise beyond failure

Shape yourself to smile through your tears

Shape yourself to love beyond measure

Shape yourself to be the best you can be

Shape yourself to start afresh when all seems in vain

Shape yourself to NEVER NEVER NEVER give up

Shape yourself to run your race

Shape yourself to understand others needs

Shape yourself to embrace change

As you shape yourself to greatness, you will have shaped the life you have and who you are.

Live The Race to The Finish

We are all in a race, we are chasing our dreams, and we are chasing our goals too. Determination and courage are the key to reaching out to where we want to be. There is nothing easy in this world, yet, there is nothing impossible as well. If we dream it, then we can achieve it. If you think you can, nothing should ever stand in your way. We live only once, make the most of it by always finishing what you have started. If you managed to take off, think positive, stay focused and be sure of landing. The sky may be rough, with thunders and storms everywhere but HOLD ON. There is no rose without thorns. A lot of people give up in the middle of their journey, after they have sacrificed a lot. It's never worth it giving up anything, no wonder they say, NEVER GIVE UP, even when the ends do not meet, just know that a smile is coming through and it is just at the corner.

Perseverance is a key to success. It is not always about reaching the destination first, sometimes it is all about just reaching there.

In 1968, Tanzania made a history in the marathon that took place in Mexico city. A history that has built generations to believe in never giving up, to have patience and persistence.

John Stephen Akhwari (born 1938 in Mbulu, Tanganyika) is a former Tanzanian marathon runner. He represented Tanzania in the marathon at the 1968 Summer Olympics in Mexico City. A young, brave and athletic man, from northern Tanzania with a dream of becoming a winner in the Olympics marathon, came out to be the last but the best last. He was running to be a winner when he fell, badly cutting his knee and dislocating the joint. He was given first aid and it was concluded that he should be taken to the hospital but he refused and instead, kept running to finish his race.

One hour later, as the crowd was leaving the stadium and the winner of the marathon had been announced, John Steven Akhwari appeared in the stadium. He was overwhelmed with pain in every step, hardly walking, hardly running. His leg bloodied and bandaged. Despite the pain, he kept running towards the finish line. He didn't give up, he never gave up. The sun had set when Akhwari crossed the finish line and the small crowd gave him a cheer.

Later on, a reporter asked Akhwari why he continued with the race while he had no chance of winning. , He said, "My country did not send me [here] to start the race, they sent me to finish the race." Since then he has become an Olympic legend.

You Master Plan Your Life

Life has only one formula, the one you put to it, to calculate risks, add happiness, subtract stress, multiply peace and divide sorrow.

Life has no meaning but the meaning you derive from it.

Life gives every human being a priority of being the master planner of their own routes, and their own lives.

It is not a surprise finding our lives in the hands of other people, our friends, family and partners and we totally lose control and focus on our inner goals of life.

Many people are living to achieve someone else's goal in their lifetime. They forget that each life has a purpose, a goal to reach out to and each soul is the master planner and achiever of its own goals in life.

Mimicking lifestyles and behaviour deprive ourselves away from the master plan we owe to have.

If life was a bus, you are the driver

If life was a plane, you are the pilot

If life was a ship, you are the captain

Take a position in your life, to engrave and walk in the direction of your master plan. No one can drive you away from your own goals or put you down but yourself.

Failure starts when we put our lives on hold and start living someone else's life.

Setting Goals

I remember when I was young, older people would constantly ask me, who I would want to be when I grow up. I had always said I wanted to be a doctor. I look back at those old beautiful days when I was just an innocent child and I realize I have not been who I said and dreamed I would become when I grow up.

Many of us, change dreams and careers because our preferences have changed, the life we have adopted, our attitudes have changed and sometimes we change for no good reason at all. We have had dreams ever since we were young, the question is, are we sitting on our dreams that we barely let them pave way to the universe or we dare to walk beyond the dream world?

All in all, we have goals to achieve as we change our dreams to a reality. Your goals in life will lead you, direct you and take you to where you want to be only if you work hard in accomplishing them.

We have to nurture our dreams, talents, goals and strategies to achieve it all.

Dream, believe, achieve and inspire generations.

Plan Your Tomorrow

The sun rises to renew people's lives, give them new hope in life and lead them to better days. The sun rises to renovate the spirit within us.

Life is full of challenges, ups and downs, so many mountains to climb and rivers to cross. At times, life is like the sun shining on top of our heads, at noon, making us busy looking for a shade, a comfort from an excessive heat. Life is beautiful but the path through it is never smooth. The most important thing is to realize who you are, where you are from and where you are going. Analyze the choices and decisions you make every day in your life.

When the sun sets every evening, it is a moment to evaluate our day, the challenges we have faced and plan for tomorrow.

You Cannot Reverse Today

Today is a beautiful gift of life we have ever had, tomorrow is not guaranteed, a story yet to be told.

Time wasted today will not have room for compensation in the future. Do not get stuck in the world of tomorrow and put to death your today. It is today that will give you something to talk and refer to when tomorrow comes. If you do not have anything worth talking about yesterday, then what will your tomorrow be like if you live today like yesterday?

Do not imprison yourself in the world of tomorrow, get out of that shell and live your life, today is the only day you have to do one and do it all. Anything that you are set to achieve, work on it today and start taking baby steps now so that by sunset, you are able to walk on your own.

Move Out of Your Comfort Zone

- There is always a new challenge, grab it
- Expand your understanding of success
- Think positive and keep climbing the mountain of your life with hope and faith for a better day
- Keep learning daily
- Do something new
- Go for more adventures in life
- Keep working on your abilities and desires
- Move to a higher target
- Change lives of others who are not as lucky as you
- Move out of your comfort zone

Learning From Our Mistakes

We are human, we are not angels and we are bound to make a lot of mistakes in our lives. The question to ask ourselves is, do we learn from our mistakes or do we keep repeating the same mistakes over and over again?

Imagine if in every single minute of your life you are doing an exam and you forget to write your name or examination number. If you forget once, it is easy for people to understand but if you keep on forgetting every time then people will surely think there is something wrong with you and that you just don't learn from your mistakes.

When a person keeps repeating the same mistake, then people do not see that as a mistake anymore.

It is OK to make mistakes but it is not OK to repeat the same mistake. Many times, mistakes are a result of bad decisions that we make in our endeavours. Making right decisions help to eliminate chances of making mistakes. No one can ever influence decision making in your life, You are your own boss; you are your own leader. You have to understand that, the decisions you make will have an impact on your daily routines, your relationships and your future as well. If you make bad decisions, then the risk of a mistake occurring is big and if you make good decisions, you lessen the chances of making mistakes.

Presidents, CEOs, Pastors, Sheikh, Professors, Doctors, Pilots, Engineers and even presidents, make mistakes, who are you not to? The only thing that will differentiate you positively from others is learning from your mistakes and leading a way to create a brighter future for yourself, your country and the world at large.

Learning from your mistakes will always drive you to the next level and it is a doorway to success.

Let A Smile Enrich Your Life

A smile is a perfect gift you can give to yourself and it will help you decrease stress and enjoy life, one day at a time. I always feel so much satisfaction once I see a child smiling for a child's smile is as pure as his thoughts destined to enrich lives. It is always genuine and from the heart. It eases the soul from all the struggles of the world.

Possess a child's smile always. It is a light in moments of darkness, quenches your heart's thirst for happiness, enrich lives and it is the best medicine for the soul's weakness.

Smile through thunders and storms, smile through sunshine and rain, smile through moonlight and dark night, smile in between love and hate, smile through mountains to climb and rivers to cross.

Smile and keep smiling throughout your life.

Do Your Best

Thirteen years ago, my primary school teacher, taught me a song that has been a backbone of everything I do in my life. I wish I could sing it for you as you are reading this precious book. The lyrics of the song are as follow:

Do your best and God will do the rest

No sweat, no sweet

For nothing, nothing comes

Do not keep till tomorrow what can be done today

First thing first

Discipline and efforts belong together

Be the way of whatever you are

It is not about the tune of the song, rather it is the lyrics in it. They are so powerful to lift up your world. Ever since I learnt that song, my perception to life changed and every day I live within those lines.

Sing at your own tune. Make it your motto in life. And let your world be colourful.

Go For What You Want

There is nothing easy in this world and there is nothing impossible as well. Most of the times, when you are just about to give up, miracles happen. I don't know if you do believe in miracles or not, personally, I do. I have seen miracles in my life.

In March 2011, I could hardly smile without feeling a hot nail stubbing my heart. Life was not fun anymore. Days were dull; nights were long and full of nightmares. I could not understand how things were happening.

Every fibre in my body felt like it was time for me to lose hope. It was time for me to give up and settle for less. I did not dare let hope walk through that door I refused to give up. I refused to lose. I remembered, victory never comes instantly, it is a journey. I told myself, I may lose the battle, but I am going to win the war.

One month before being admitted at the University for my Second Degree, I got a job at a multinational corporation in marketing and sales department. Few weeks after I joined the organization, I got a letter of admission, from the University of Dar es Salaam, informing me that I had been selected to join the University for Master's degree in the business school and the fee for the program was USD8040. Unfortunately, I was not on the list of students who got scholarship. At that moment, I knew I wanted to study. Many people advised me to wait for another year and see if I can get scholarship but my mind was set on studying the same year and not another year. The motivation of studying that I had may never be there in the following year. I decided to quit my job for school.

I had a task of raising money for school fees, to pay and get registered. I had only two weeks to raise money and between me and poverty I had 100,000 TZS only. I wanted to study, but I had no money. I asked myself, should I just give up education because I have no money for school fees?! And the answer was NO. Every time I asked myself that question, the answer was NO, NEVER GIVE UP.

I started attending classes while looking for financial support for my first module and registration. I decided to request different people, family and friends, for financial support. Together with my friend, who also did not get scholarship, we got four thousand dollars; two thousand dollars each.

Within twenty four hours of having that money, as I was going to the bank, I lost my wallet and when I found it, there was everything else except the money. It was the hardest period of my life. Just as I thought I had got school fees, to start with, I lost all the money, only two days were left for registration and I was back to square one.

My friend, with whom we had raised money together, had 2000 USD with her and she gave me 1000 USD so that I can get registered for my studies while seeking financial support. For four months, I was at school, studying full time, with no scholarship or any financial support and life was hard every day. With every sunrise, I believed in every dark hour, that there was a ray of light penetrating. You can decide to be negative and fall on the dark hour or be positive and live in that ray of light which shines.

I didn't have any income at all but I did not lose hope in looking for full scholarship for my studies. At that time my first priority was getting done with my studies whether I had to stay the whole day at the university without eating because I didn't have money or wait for my friend's lift to go back home because I didn't have bus fare. Giving up was not an option at all.

In July 2011, I got full scholarship for my studies and now I am a holder of Masters degree in International Business.

If you know what you want at a certain moment of your life, do not hesitate, do not look back, go for what you want as long as it yields better and not bitter results.

The beginning may be very rough, you may have sleepless nights, countless thoughts, no single cent in your wallet and everyone looking at you as if you are confused but that is never a reason for you to give up. You are your own life's architect.

A Heart To Love

Would you prefer to love or to hate? Some people prefer to LOVE. Love brings happiness, joy to the heart and a life free of regrets but full of contentment. Love brings a smile when we wake up in the morning, Love teaches us to think of others before ourselves, love brings harmony, peace and unity. Love does not create enemies. Love finds you where you are and brightens up your life.

Some people would rather HATE. If you think that is better in your case, do you ask yourself why each morning when you wake up, you have a frowning face, you yell at people, you have bad attitude towards things and people as well, you just can't handle someone standing in your way. Your heart is full of anger and resentment, you don't find perfect peace, and you are busy pretending you are happy. You think you are living a good life through hating one another, because they did this or the other. You are just hurting yourself. Can't you see you are damaging your heart? It is too fragile for what you are putting it through.

A heart is a source of all evils and a heart is a source of all good, the choice is yours, to fill it with what you see fit.

A Beautiful Struggle

Victory comes to those who work hard, who struggle to be where they want to be. It is a beautiful struggle when you work so hard, sweat all over, and you find sweet victory, you reap what you sow.

Every hard work eventually pays off. Every sweat will eventually be replaced with a sweet fragrance. If you are head over heels in the struggle for success, victory will knock at your door. It is a beautiful struggle to be where you are and move to where you want to be. It is a beautiful struggle.

Life In A Corner

There are moments in our lives when we feel like the whole world is against us and we hardly breathe happiness. To us, life becomes a challenge. Our plans are destructed. Our lives are at a corner, like a pill, too bitter to swallow. At that very moment, the world seems too selfish and everyone is against you.

You are unique and special in this world. You deserve to be happy and live your dreams. You deserve the best of life. Happiness is found from within you, within yourself. When you are at a corner, and nothing real seem like working, just put your head up and tell yourself, you are better than all the challenges and however low they will bring you, you are going to rise beyond it all.

Never let challenges of life drive you crazy. Stand strong through it all and smile even when going through bitterness. If you let the world drive you around then you will never find your place and position in the universe. Before you add up anything in your life, heartaches and confusion, know that you are special and the best thing that has ever happened in this world.

Everyone was created special and unique each in their own way, treat yourself as such. Treat yourself as special before anyone else does. Find happiness in yourself, accept the challenges and smile.

The Living Hope

As long as we are humans, there are a lot of times we have broken hearts and we face situations that test our patience. We should let hope be our soul food. Broken hearts should not bring broken strings of hope.

All happens for a reason, everything. Dinner time will never come unless you have endured the burning sun during the day. Like Clifford Harris said, sometimes you got to go through hell just to get to heaven, but no matter what, keep standing tall. In your situation, don't look down on yourself, live a life of making a difference in the world, in you and to other people as well. Learn from each situation that God puts in your life. Laugh, it's the best medicine.

Whatever that is going on in your life, you are the one to give meaning to it, positive or negative. Live a positive life knowing that

God is in control of everything that you are going through. You were born a winner, so smile through it all. You might think you have lost something, but look on both sides of a coin, you might have gained a greater lesson that the one you lost.

You are serving a purpose on this earth. You are not here accidentally and whatever happens to you happens for a reason, to give a deeper meaning to your life.

Time

Many of us do not like at all being reminded l about time. We like to do things our way with no pressure. We pull up blankets when it is too cold and we stay late watching a movie and get too tired for work the next day. We do not like to be told "you are late" yet we don't make efforts to be in time. We like to be told, job well done, yet we don't make efforts to work on our tasks and responsibilities before the deadline is around the corner.

Tick tock tick tock, you know we all have only 24 hours in a day. From the billionaires, presidents, nurses, beggars, we all have the same time to use, spend and make the most of it in a day. The hard part is, how do you use your time??? Some use it to hustle and be millionaires, some to move from millionaires to billionaires, some to bring peace in their countries, some to help the poor, some to take care of the sick, to build a better nation.

Every being has to be responsible in time management. Planning accordingly, being at an appointment, meeting, conference, church, mosque etc. at the right time that everyone expects you to be.

Time is never to be taken for granted. The way we have managed time is a great measure of our success and failure.

Ask yourself, how do you spend your time?!

Patience

In life, I learned that nothing comes so easy, almost all things need you to wait, and the results are always worth waiting for.

Patience is the fruit of the spirit. Patience will take you places and patience will help you see your dreams come to reality.

Success does not come instantly. Many times people pass through the failure, heartbreak, disasters, hatred and a very bad moment before they see a breakthrough in their lives.

Patience will give you strength to conquer hardships in life. A person without patience is like a well without water.

Stand On Your Own

Every morning, as the sun rises, what thoughts come to your head? When you are faced with difficult decisions, where do you look up to? Every single day that passes by, what do you live for? At a position you are this very moment, are you there so that you can please someone or just yourself? Are you doing things because your father, mother, spouse or a friend told you to do so or because of self-motivation?

I remember, back in 2003, when I got my form four NECTA results and got a first division, I was selected in the best girls' school in Tanzania which was known for admitting girls who had performed very well in their previous levels of education. After a smooth one year at school, I fell sick and had a minor surgery which later on had some complications which led me to go through five months of healing. This caused me to lag behind in my studies. At the age of 17, I made up my mind that staying at that school was not a good idea for me and would not lead me to the success that I yearned for. I told my family and relatives of my decision to move to another school that I wanted but none gave me the support I needed and the only thing I could hear day and night was, "you are at the best girls school", yet I didn't feel that way. I knew staying in that school would not give me the results I yearned for, and had always dreamed of.

One beautiful day, I decided to stand on my own, I decided to take the bull by its horns. Decisions had to be made for I was not going to study by pleasing my family and relatives; rather, I was studying for my life, a better life. Someone once said, "Failure begins when you start pleasing everyone."

I took a step further and sent an application letter to a school I wanted to study, then I made follow ups. Later on, I was called for an interview, I told my mother and she then gave me all the support I needed. I then joined the other school which was almost 1200 miles away from home. It was in that school that I knew my goal would be reached.

I kept on climbing the ladder of success. My sight was towards the peak, so beautiful, and I wanted to be there.

In April 2006, I was amongst the students who got a first class in science subjects in the Advanced level exams. I look back at my life, and I know, if I was not strong enough to go for what I wanted and stand on my own, I would not have gotten the results I did.

In all your ways, do not live to please others you will end up a failure. Make decisions, but make them right. Take calculated risks and be yourself.

A Friend's Love

I remember when I was in standard six; I had a nose bleeding problem. One afternoon after dispersing from school assembly ground, nose bleeding started profusely. All my efforts to stop it could not work.

A friend of mine, Luciana, eleven years old like me, came over and told me to lean forward while she squeeze the soft part of my nose until the blood stopped. It was amazing. I didn't know she could be a doctor in a minute. I was puzzled and very thankful.

That was an act of love. The love that she had for me led her to do things just to make sure that I become OK and I could look up and smile again.

A true friend's love is pure. She/he is on your side at all times, supporting you, lifting you up, sharing ugly and good moments, loving you with all your faults, does not envy and does not count the wrongs.

A true friend's love is as deep as the ocean. She/he will stand by you when you are weak and will warn you when you are leading to a wrong road. She/he will sail with you in storms and thunders.

Do you love your friends so much that you would make sure you take away their pain and give them a sweet smile on their faces? Love your friends, love your family and love your neighbours, it is the beginning of wisdom.

Determination

If the whole world had determination and perseverance as much as a baby has, we would all be in a better place. Have you ever seen babies learning to walk? They always fall down so many times, at first even standing on their own is so hard, but with determination, they stand on their two feet even if it means standing up for few seconds before they fall down on their back. Slowly but still with determination, they start taking baby steps, one step at a time and at the end of it all, after countless falling down and using the tables and walls as their support, finally they walk on their own. They never give up. They have a strong will and determination.

Life is just like taking baby steps. There are so many times we will fall down, hurt ourselves, need support but it is the determination within us that enables us to walk again, to stand upright and look back at all the baby steps we took, the challenges we faced and to be proud of ourselves. It is never easy, but with determination, you can do and be whatever you want to do.

Giving Is An Art

Why should you receive every day? What are you giving back to your family, your friends, your community and your country? Look around and think of your life, how many people have enriched your life, empowered you with good education, supported your career, filled your soul with courageous words, surrounded your daily activities with peace and love? Should you only receive? Look around again, how many people are less fortunate than you? How many people would love to be where you are but they have no means to do that? How many people in your community can't afford even a daily meal, good education and shelter? Should you only receive? Have you ever asked yourself, what do these people living in difficult conditions receive? Have you ever thought of giving so that they may receive just as much as you also receive?

They say if you want to enjoy life and live in peace and complete happiness, give. You don't have to be rich to give; you just have to have a heart ready to serve other people.

We give to enrich other people's lives, to empower them and to brighten up their faces with a beautiful smile. The more you give, the more you receive. Giving is an art, you can sing it, you can play it, you can dance it, you can paint it, and you can write it. Giving is an art!

Keep Climbing

Mountains resemble the challenges we are facing in life, the ups and downs, trials and triumphs. Just like climbing a mountain, life is not a rehearsal. Health specialists always advise us to be prepared at least two months before climbing a mountain through exercising and knowing your body health status. If you are not prepared, there is one percent chance that you will reach the peak. Life is just like mountain climbing. If you do not get yourself prepared to live and reach the peak of your career or anything that you do want to achieve in your life, you will end up being a dreamer always.

When climbing mountains, you pass through steep valleys as well as deep forests, and there a lot of times you will hesitate to go on climbing, asking yourself why you ever decided go up the mountain. Push on, a time will come that you lift up your head and have the view of the peak, you will have strength to conquer the mountain.

In life, with a goal that you have set to achieve, there will be a lot of challenges that may draw you back if you are not careful. It is never easy to achieve a goal you have set for yourself, it requires a lot of sacrifice and the sweat you will pour out, will always be worth it.

Life is like climbing a mountain; it is never easy, but worth the efforts if you do not give up. The biggest challenge is, once you reach one peak, there are always other mountains and peaks to reach.

Keep climbing

The Past

Time flies and soon we realize the bad decisions we have made, the routes that we had chosen do not put a smile on our faces. Some call it the past, some call it history and some put it all together as the history about the past.

One day as I was reflecting on some of the decisions that I made in my life, I felt bitter and thought of all the time wasted. I asked myself only one question, "Is there any reason to be bitter about the past?" I kept meditating on my life and realized if it was not for my past failures and mistakes, I would not have enough room to gain more knowledge and grow positively towards the light of success. It was then I decided to write a poem:

My past has shaped me,
My mistakes have taught me,
My dark spots have designed me,
The journey I travelled has sharpened me,
The road I took, has directed me,
People I met have defined me,
People I let go have identified me,
Decisions I made have constructed me,
Mountains I climbed have toned me,
Rivers I crossed have taught me how to swim,
Music I danced has given me a beat to ma life.

A minute ago, is part of the past that we have lived. Everything that we go through in our lives is a measure of wisdom and courage filling our days. A beautiful part of yesterday is that it is past, it is gone already and we have today to thank yesterday for shaping us to who we are, recognizing the right and the wrong. Every minute that we live, we are shaping our past, our present and our future. That night, I concluded writing my thoughts in three lines only:

My life has shaped me,
My life is a song I compose every day,
My life is a song I perfect every day.

Rules For Yourself

The country has rules and regulations that govern it, tribes have customs people abide to, families have rules they live by, schools and universities have regulations, work places and leisure related places have rules. The only thing we forget is having ground rules for ourselves.

We live to follow different rules that we forget to create and implement our own rules. Some of the rules you can have in life are the following:

To live to the fullest every day that passes by

To never regret the past but to learn from it

To never to give up or give in

To love with all your heart

To analyse every situation in life

To be patient

To know that there is a higher power

To always be positive

To understand that there is nothing impossible in this world

To be whoever you want to be

To do whatever you want to do

To always stand up for what you believe in

To cherish friendship

To follow your dreams

To cultivate your talents

To be happy no matter the situation

To understand there is a reason for everything in life

Make your personal rules to follow. You choose the life that you want to live, life does not choose you.

Reverse Roles

I had never seen my mom sick in bed until when I was 25 years old. It was at that moment when the alarm clock rang and reminded me of the aging process that both my mom and I have undergone.

Our parents and guardians have been taking care of us for years and years ever since we were born. Time passes by and we keep growing from a boy to a man and from a girl to a woman. Our parents and guardians grow older every passing day and as they grow older they move from being independent to being dependent and we, as children, we move from being dependent on them to being independent. At that moment, the roles between a parent and a child reverse.

Many people do not know that our parents do take care of us and it will reach a point we will have to take care of them.

Time does not reverse. We were once children and with time we become old men and women.

Be ready and be prepared for responsibilities in your life. Look at your parents or guardians now and do realize that, soon you will be exchanging shoes. Play your part right.

There is a quote by Kheri Mbiro which says, "My heart and life would have been empty, hollow if I did not experience love. I was born with my heart and not short of feelings; but maturity of the love that I feel has filled the void that has always been in me, and completed me. My heart, my love has graduated."

Chapter 5

Maturity and A World Beyond Words

The Nation Within You

By: Modesta L. Mahiga

"Anyone can count the seeds in an apple, but only God can count the number of apples in a seed." – Robert H. Schuller.

The Danger of Potential

One of the most disappointing things to experience is to watch how someone gets smug and content to hear that they have "potential". "Potential" my friends, is deceiving; it can lull you into a slumber even as you walk in wakefulness. "Potential" lures you into a false sense of confidence and security as you say to yourself "I've got it in me, it's just waiting for the right time to come before I use it." Newsflash: settling for the fact that there is latent "potential" in you is the most dangerous and debilitating disease you could suffer from.

"Potential" is described in the Oxford dictionary as "having or showing the capacity to develop into something in the future", "latent [(of a quality or state) existing but not yet developed or manifest; hidden or concealed – lying dormant or hidden until circumstances are suitable for development or manifestation] qualities or abilities that may be developed and lead to future success or usefulness"; "the possibility of something happening or of someone doing something in the future."

Potential says you have greatness in you and there is a possibility that someday, somehow, you could become those things, maybe, there is a possibility. Potential cripples you and makes you complacent because potential tells you to wait for tomorrow and we all know that tomorrow never comes.

They say that a graveyard is the wealthiest place in the world. This is not because people are buried with great treasures in their caskets but because people are the treasure buried in graves.

Because we continue to wait for our "potential" to be realized tomorrow, many people die with "potential" to have changed their circumstances and the very environment they lived in. Because they did not pursue their potential to its end, at the end it died with them forever remaining "potential" unrealized.

So many unwritten books, untold stories, un-invented creations, unrealized dreams, unsung heroes go to the grave with a wealth of talent and solutions to their and the world's challenges. Solutions that the world will never enjoy the benefit of because the one person they could have come from settled for having the "potential" to make a difference instead of unleashing what was only "potential" to what is "kinetic" energy – "energy which a body possesses by virtue of being in motion".

Potential in Motion

The difference between potential and kinetic energy is that whilst the former is harnessed in a reservoir and could do great things once released, until then it remains untapped, dormant, useless; the latter however, is energy that is conquering fear, moving, doing, daring, now. Kinetic energy is energy created because of movement, not lying dormant in potential. Kinetic energy moves, flows in the present, continuously; being used now, energy generated and applied now to build, strengthen, add value.

The upside of having potential however, is the fact that you have something (as opposed to having nothing and we know that God gave every single person something to start with); to have potential means there is greatness in you that is dying to be unleashed, to be released, to be made known to the world, to bring change, to make a difference.

Tanzanian Youth unlock Tanzania's Potential

Tanzania is like a 50-year old person with "potential". Imagine living to 50 and people around you still speak of you as having "potential". 50 and you haven't lived out your best life, when do you think you'll start, at 100?

Tanzania is the second most naturally endowed country in the world, it has the highest free-standing mountain in the world, it has the largest fresh water lake in the world, it has the second largest lake in the world, the second deepest lake in the world, the largest Game Reserve in the world, national parks with the highest number and diversity of the Big Five animals in the world, the second highest waterfall in Africa, the second largest number of UNESCO World Heritage Sites in Africa, rich minerals and gemstones, including Tanzanite which is only found in Tanzania, peace, unity, a common language, large population, access to 20% of the world's water and the list goes on and on.

Like seeds in an apple, Tanzania's known features give it great hidden potential. How many apples will come out of the seeds we can count as Tanzania's assets, only God knows and only Tanzanian youth, in whose hands Tanzania's future lies, can realize.

Tanzanian youth are the seeds in an apple called Tanzania. You can count how many youth we have but, the potential of what could come out of us only God knows.

Tanzania is blessed beyond measure, Tanzanian youths already have the capital in the country and themselves, to do great things; what we need to do is shirk away the fallacy that we will realize our potential "when we grow older", "when we earn a lot of money", "when we are in positions of power", "when the country changes", because "we are the people we have been waiting for, we are the change that we seek" and the time is now. Like apple seeds, we already have every single thing we need to become great apple trees, bearing even more apples with even more seeds and even more apples etcetera.

Make a Difference Now

Like kinetic energy, let us move now, and not wait with our potential until 'circumstances are right'. It is only by making a move now and starting with the gifts and talents that God has placed in our hands that we will be given more to manage, and as we accomplish our assignment at a lower level, that a greater challenge will be posed that we can solve at the next, and so we grow and our country develops.

I am sure we are all familiar with the famous story of Moses and the Israelites. God asked Moses to lead and to take the Israelites out of captivity in Egypt but Moses was not willing to do this. He kept on making excuses for what he did not have, for what he could not do; he had speech impediment, he had killed someone, he didn't live like an Israelite, he was away from his people for a very long time and so they didn't know him etcetera but God asked him: "what is it that is in your hand?" – God was saying to Moses, you already have everything you need to live a life of success and significance; start with what you have and I will bring you the people and resources to support you on your journey but, by all means Moses, start! When Moses finally realized that no one else was going to come to improve his life and the life of his people, he was willing to go and, as soon as he had made up his mind to stand in the gap, God brought him people and resources and God Himself was with Moses as he fought adversity, released his people from captivity and lead them to the promised land.

It is only when we are "sick and tired of being sick and tired" and feel "enough is enough" and say "here I am, I am ready to do something constructive and ethical to change my life and that of our people" that we will find that God will bring us the people and resources to realize our dreams. I don't know what "Egypt" is standing in your way, I don't know what your fears are, I don't know what the "promised land" is to you and the people you want to "lead out" but you already have in your hand, in you, what it takes to take the first step to that desired destination and, God will meet you in your readiness.

We are the Ones We Have Been Waiting For

If we wait for an "enabling environment" or "favourable conditions" before we make a move to improve our livelihood, our community's welfare, our Nation's development, we may find that the "enabling environment" and "favourable conditions" are never coming. As a matter of fact, it should come as no surprise to us when we tell God that we were waiting for Him to intervene in our favour in Tanzania, to hear Him say that He was waiting for us to show willingness to stand in the gap for our families, community, nation; to take the first step to create our own "enabling environment", create our own "favourable conditions" before He revealed to us the next stage of the journey and sent each of us the people and resources we would need to make it through.

Reposition for Take Off

So what does it take to stand and be counted? To realize otherwise hidden potential in us as Tanzanian youths in this great, fertile and rich apple that is Tanzania?

- Know, build a relationship with and trust God
- Know who you are
- Value what you're worth of
- Know Tanzania's great wealth
- Take pride in being Tanzanian
- Decide where you're going
- Choose how you will get there
- Investing in sustained, long-term benefits
- Have patience
- Have no fear

These are all choices we will have to make, we choose to be the best we can be, we choose to love our Country, we choose to focus on the future instead of feeding out stomachs in the short-term, we choose to feel the fear and do it anyway. It all rests in you choosing what is best for you, your family, your community, your Country. It is in continuing to choose what is best which will determine our ultimate success and significance, improving the livelihood of our people, driving Tanzania's economic independence and its social development.

Repeat these steps over and over and over and over and over again at each stage of your journey as you unleash your potential to drive your life, that of your family and community, Nation and this very world to greater heights; keeping your eyes focused on Christ, focused on fulfilling your God-given purpose, playing the role that only you were born to play in

Tanzania's emancipation, knowing that the potential lying dormant in you has the power, when put into action, to transform not only you, your family, your community, your Nation but this very world we live in.

You see, "anyone can count the seeds in an apple, but only God can count the number of apples in a seed"; no one but God knows the great person you can become, the great things you could do, the great relief you could bring this troubled world but, you hold all power to decide whether you will allow yourself, putting away all fear, all doubt, shutting out all noise and negative advice to stand willing, ready and available to be used as a channel to pass all the hidden wealth and potential in yourself and this Nation, to meet a need that only you and Tanzania were created to fulfill for this generation and the nation within you that is to come.

Achieving Your Dreams

By: Flaviana Matata

To achieve your dreams needs primarily focus with clear determination. Do not let anyone tell you that your dream is too big, less ambitious, too unrealistic, not suited to your personality etc. Often times when we dream we look at the end product but anything is achievable, however, we always have to start somewhere.

If you decide for example that you want to be an international model, then, look for opportunities, and be prepared. Being prepared in this case means, ensuring that you are in good shape, you have a healthy skin and teeth, you have the right height, clean and strong hair and nails. So it doesn't matter if you achieve your dream in 10 years' time, but you have to be prepared from day 1. When it comes to finding opportunities, always look at anything that comes your way and ask if that is another opportunity to increase your knowledge and experience and if that experience will make you better and stronger in the future.

The other important element is discipline. You have to be consistent and never waiver in your decisions. Even when you are going through rough times, stay focused and keep your faith that you will achieve finally what you want. If you give up and resort to eating and partying for example, it means that you are setting yourself back in achieving your goal to be an international model. A good example is before I started my career, I never used to drink alcohol and I still don't drink alcohol.

Finally it is important to always important to analyse yourself and see whether the path you are taking is directing you towards your career. Occasional balanced and objective assessment is a good way of ensuring that you do not deviate unnecessarily from your dream career.

Goals In Life: My Winning Approach

By: Lusajo L. Mwaisaka

The first half of 2011 taught me only one thing, I am stronger than the trials and tribulations I am set to face in my lifetime. More than once, giving up was the best offer on the table and at times the only way out for me was to accept it all and live with defeat in my heart. Through the ups and downs, I found peace that made me regain control of my life and helped me in setting my goals straight.

Plans of a man are many and more than once they collide with plans that God has in store for us. When dreams were shattered it took every ounce of energy in me to bounce back and move on without loss of enthusiasm. And here I am, planning to win and the sure way to win is to survive in this world. Disappointments and grief are our own to deal with and the choice is ours; to let them pull us down or to get back up.

Life on Earth is temporary for I believe we die every day we go to sleep. Every new dawn is the first day of the rest of your life; a gift that God saw you fit to be granted the present moment, today. There is a quote from a song saying, "The game of life is the struggle to survive, we live to win because if we lose we die" and also I remember another line from a song saying "Life has no mean; we were all born to die so no screams." When you look at the two it is easy to say that we are all born losers for every living soul shall surely taste death. Then what makes you a winner?

"A winner is someone who recognizes his/her God-given talents, works his/her tail off to develop them into skills, and uses these skills to accomplish his/her goals – Larry Bird."

Strive to realize your goals in life, keeping in mind that nothing is permanent, even those things that hurt the most, work towards achieving your goals. Live in such a way that when your number is called, you will continue living in the hearts of people you have touched during your lifetime.

"I can't change the direction of the wind, but I can adjust my sails to always reach my destination"

You Can Be Whatever You Want To Be

By: Folawe- 'Femi Banigbe

As a little young girl, life seemed very exciting. I loved playing with my brothers and sisters and friends in the neighbourhood. I loved to sing and also loved reading nice stories at a very young age. As a family we would sit outside under the bright moon and sparkling stars and sing favourite rhymes and lullabies. As a young teenager, I discovered that through the rough times that we started going through as a result of hardships in the family and in the nation, I still found so much pleasure in a number of things. I loved to read; I admired older women who stood up for their society and helped people, when I sang people told me I had a great voice. I joined the school and church choir; I loved to know what the human body was all about and read so much about it. It didn't take me quite long in life before I knew what I wanted to be later on in life. At first I loved the thought of being a medical doctor but later on I realized that wasn't what I wanted. I ended up with a school degree in the medical line and I loved it. I started writing about myself and environment and I never stopped thinking about who I wanted to be and how to get there. Even though, there was so much distractions as time went on, I would get myself back in line and review my goals and dreams. I knew who I was, I discovered what I liked and I put much effort in the things that seemed quite easy for me to achieve. And so here I am today, a woman on a mission, speaking up for other women just like I saw women do when I was young. I am a publisher of a health magazine that helps women to prepare for pregnancy and parenting, I am a mother of two lovely kids and I have a foundation that helps reduce maternal mortality and infant death in Africa. I still love singing and I have written quite a number of songs.

Dear one, I am not where I want to be yet but I am surely not where I used to be! Life has not been all rosy and sweet but I have managed to land on my feet mostly because I have a dream and a creator who has kept and sustained me. You can be ALL you want to be and you can have it all regardless of your history or background. Most success stories you read all the time come from the most unlikely ones to have them and you wonder why they do have a success story? It is simply because they never give up. Everyone wants to be rich and famous and live the most comfortable lives ever but the ones who have good reason for being wealthy are the ones it happens for most! Now I am not talking about luck or some sort of voodoo to amass wealth. Anyone who has truly been wealthy by the good reasons and lived in peace with it (that which money cannot buy) are those who have lived for a vision bigger than themselves. For instance, if your dream is to take all under privileged children off the streets and to stop child labour in Africa, that is a great vision and for every vision, there is PRO-vision. This provision would come in form of ideas and great opportunities for which you must have prepared yourself for and they will come to you. When you are diligent and hold on to your dreams, you will find yourself with great minds like you who will believe in your dreams and help you make your dreams come true. Soon afterwards you will realize that real dreamers do not stay in bed; they get up and live their dreams.

So you might ask, "I don't even know what I want to become". Then let ask me you? What makes you happy, makes you sit still and listen or even makes you cry? What are the problems you see in your environment or school or even in the nation that makes you angry or ask so many questions? These might be signs of what you have been called to be, to do for your community or solve for your generation. Also the things you find very easy to achieve are important signs too. What you need to do NOW is get a small notebook and write a short description of whom you are and what you like. Write out all the things you would love to be in the future and how you plan to contribute to your great country. Note that life is not about being popular but being relevant. Most of the people in government in many African countries today are popular but not relevant just because they live very selfish lives and do not care about the Nation they are supposed to be serving. You must choose which one you want; popularity or relevance and help to your society. When you desire a live of service, you have chosen a life that is bigger than you and you will realize that you have a vision and hence provision for this vision will come to you. The best place to invest is in people's hearts and whatever you do will live on as stories that people will tell. Choose that kind of life today young one and you will soon discover that you can be all that you want to be!

Train Yourself To Be A Leader

By: Richard Kasesela

I was always an admirer of JF Kennedy's quote "My fellow citizens of the world, ask not what America will do for you, but what together we can do for the freedom of man". This quote helped me to keep on as a mantra whereby, whenever I am given a role as a leader this quote comes back to me. It is true, if we are chosen as leaders we should always try to evaluate ourselves on what can we do for the nation. This internal analysis has helped me to stop putting blame for bad happenings, rather, trying to find solutions. It has been common for most of us either to blame our parents, the government or even our friends for what is happening to us rather than putting our strength in looking at the root cause and seek the better solution. The young upcoming leaders should always ask what they can do for their country and not what a country can do for them.

There are some incidents in life which can make you stop doing one of the important things you loved in your life. I was in standard six when one day our stream, 6C was playing against 6B. I was a defender, and when one striker was about to score while trying to defend I played so hard on him and he fell down. When I looked at his hand it was deformed and I knew right-away that it was broken. I was so scared. That was the end of me playing soccer and since then I have only remained a football fan.

Despite what happened years back, we are still friends though he still has a scar on his hand and I have a scar in my heart for having to quit one of the best games I had ever loved. Who knows, maybe I would have been playing for the national team by now. The key thing here is that you may plan to become someone at your childhood but circumstances may push you away from your original desire or wish. This should not be taken as failure. Whatever you do now; you should do it with passion and put all your efforts and you will definitely succeed.

I started sharpening my leadership skills, ever since I was in standard one, but what helped me was the fact that I was the only child in our class at Syukula Primary school who had attended nursery school. Having studied at a Roman Catholic nursery school in Iringa gave me an added advantage of leading in class and becoming a prefect. My leadership skills got more challenged in high school as I had to contest for leadership in school prefects elections. I contested for Chief head of Food and beverages (in charge of the well-being of students at school), the role nicknamed as "mkuu wa Bwalo". It was the third top position after that of a Chair of the school and Secretary General.

The contest was tough but we all had wonderful experience during the campaigns and I eventually won with a land slide victory. What I learned from that campaigns were two things;respect all and also learn to live according to the society you want to lead. If you elevate yourself you will definitely miss a link with the people you intend to lead.

Life is full of obstacles and challenges, but the most important thing is that everyone has a chance, there are so many opportunities in the world that the whole population cannot finish them. The best and the most important thing is to do our best in whatever we do. In my life I have believed that success is brought by hard working and honesty. Good conduct plays an important role in all the achievements.

The other exciting leadership skill was at Church. I was elected a Church Councillor for four years then re-elected for another four years term. This role is usually given to older people who have tremendous leadership skills and good life conduct. I was happy and scared as I would be leading one of the prominent churches of which some of the prominent personnel both from government and private sector attend and worship. The Church leadership taught me to have maximum respect to everyone and be a good listener as the moment you ignore to listen to any one you may be costing someone's life.

I have worked in various positions. I am now chairing about 30 countries as a Chairman of Pan Africa Business Coalition. I am doing that with passion and all the commitment despite being involved in other activities. I am not saying that I have not failed, I have failed in various areas but I always use my failures as a lesson and a ladder to move to the next level. It's important to acknowledge your failure so that you can be able to work out a solution.

Life to me is full of fun, friendship and support to both sides . I sometimes agree to help to something which is difficult to achieve but I always try. One of the toughest things I try to do is when people a seeking for jobs. I will receive their résumés and start be busy with them as if I am looking for my own job. Helping others makes me feel happy and this is my benchmark of success. We are all equals what differentiates us is our efforts and attitude towards work.

In all the leadership positions I have held, I have learned that I should never negotiate with fear, fear is there to conquer.

Compromise

By: Magulya Meja Kapalata

The dignified knows what it is like to live on the streets, starved to death and unloved. May be we're not wealthy enough to adopt every child in the street, but there's a day I sympathized with a child, I put her in my arms, she clasped her tiny hands very tight round my neck and nestled on my shoulder, I could hear her heart beats humbly asking me "Is this too much to ask?". I realize we're not doing enough, if we have done anything at all. There's nothing like street children, but our sons and daughters with no safe haven

I conceded countless defeat, not only because of my wrong decisions but also by embracing wearing masks; it took me to the lowest point ever in my life. Ironically, when the deep search of my inner-self meets the being of light through faith and hope, I refuse to compromise to what I believe in. It was the turning point as it made me realize that problems are just an opinion that my decisions should reflect the sound of honour, equipment of knowledge and passion in information.

Perseverance And Endurance Equals To Success

By: Anganile T. Mwakyanjala

Born near the Indian Ocean and living near the beach for more than 20 years of my life made me fall in love with the ocean, it has always amazed me how the ocean's waves will continuously pound on the lagoon nonstop. With an ordinary mind you would ask yourself why doesn't the ocean just quit and give up because water can never push tones of rocks bordering ocean waters that have been there for centuries. However, as I grew up and during my recent visits to the ocean I realized the rocks are slowly being eaten up by the ocean and the water can reach where it couldn't same years back.! Though It has taken years but the ocean waves determination has paid off.

This is how I vowed to approach my life, whenever faced with a challenge no matter how mission impossible it might seem to any sane mind, I will always with all my strengths persevere and when my first attempt fails then I will recollect my strength to try again for perseverance is the mother of all success.

As a young person the current atmosphere in this world of recession is not favourable to our success but yet still, it is in this world that we have to put food on our plates, so one has no choice but push forward and keep pounding that rock that is the barrier to achieving our goals.

The world has been known to be the world of survival of the fittest but I would say this world is the world of survival of those who can endure. That reminds me of one of the ocean's tales that I heard from one of the beach boys that we constantly had a chat about the tales of the ocean. The story is about two fishermen who were caught in a stormy sea and their boat capsized, luckily enough they were able to hold on to the boat debris to keep them afloat, The two fishermen were in the middle of the ocean with no apparent help insight so one seeing no help in sight lost hope and instead of holding on, he said his final prayers and he let his grip off the debris and drowned. The remaining fisherman vowed to remain afloat for another 30 minutes, and when no help came he vowed to stay a little bit longer, and each time no help came he never lost hope rather he said he will keep afloat till all his strength is completely gone. After 5 hours of staying afloat a ship that was passing by came to his rescue. It was not due to his physical strength but his hope kept him alive.

The moral of the story is that, we all face struggles and challenges in our lives that in one way or the other could be similar but what determines our success or failure is the perseverance, endurance and the positive state of mind..

Have a positive mind state, look for solutions and not problems in any situation and you will always find answers to your problems and situations. Remember perseverance and endurance is the mother and father of all success.

Knowing Value and Destiny

By: Dr. Parvina Kazahura

To be able to touch someone's life, you must know the value of that life first. It's like when you want to buy something; you must look at its quality and where it was manufactured so that you are sure of what you want to buy. It is the same thing when you want to live for another's life, you must know who made them and what for? In other words, you must have a relationship with God so as to value the lives of people he created.

Touching somebody's life means giving out your energy and resources just because what you see in those lives is their destiny and not their present situation.

You cannot give what you do not have and before you have (possess), you have to be. We mostly think of doing something instead of first being somebody. You have to see it in yourself first that you are becoming somebody. You have to know who you are before you start doing something that requires you to be that person. If you want to be a doctor, you have to see yourself being a doctor before you go to a medical school otherwise there is no point in studying medicine. If you want to be a lawyer, you have to imagine yourself in the court before you go to the law school.

When you want to bring impact into other people's lives, you must see who they are, know their destiny before the process of making them or taking them to their destiny. To be able to do all that, you must love them and value their being.

Listen To Your Heart!

By: Michael Dalali

How many times do you happen to do something that comes from a push within your heart? How often do you try to listen to the inner voice rather than going with the common trend?

In life, not always are we supposed to swim according to the life trend. Not always are we to follow the common pattern.

Having a unique trend can only be realized well once one pays a great deal to his soul. Following the inner call on what to do and what do decide on. This is very important.

In critical situations, where one faces a big dilemma in life, advice given out from people around us such as friends, relatives and even our parents do act as guidance but not a call. At the end of the day in everyone's soul there happens to be a call about every crucial step we want to embark. The inner voice is a total inner call on decisions one takes. Listen to your heart.

Listening to our heart goes on even in lifelong decisions such as what kind of career path one should take, where one should go for studies or other trainings, what kind of close partners to be with which goes even further to our choices on life partners.

For example, if one wishes to take teaching as a career path in life, then he/she should stick to that call regardless of the challenges currently portrayed in the specific field.

Your heart speaks to you in the most amazing ways and in life we are faced with a challenge of listening to our hearts. It is very important to exercise the ability to trap the inner call in our souls through listening to our hearts carefully and wisely.

Rising Beyond Your Dreams

By: Nancy Lazaro

The first time I read her story through the internet I was very inspired and wanted to see her. Her life story taught me that you can be anything and anyone that you want to be, as long as you put effort into it.

I remember, it was a Friday morning when I was waiting for TEDxDAR to announce presenters for the event. Perusing over the net carefully, I came across her name, Susan Mashibe. I could not believe that finally, I was going to meet and talk to her face to face. One of the women I draw inspiration from in my life daily walk .

Self-confidence, achiever and down to earth are the characteristics of a phenomenal woman, Susan Mashibe. She carries herself with so much love and she is the only commercial pilot-cum-aircraft maintenance engineer in Tanzania. Susan is an executive director and founder of the Tanzanite Jet Centre, an aviation logistics provider to corporate, diplomatic and private jets in the region. She is the owner of Fixed Base Operation, a successful one-stop shop for private jet needs. World Economic Forum recognized her as a Young Global Leader in 2011.

Susan believes in making dreams come true. Her life is a message sent to inspire young people to reach out to their dreams despite the challenges along the way. At a tender age, she developed love for flying and started pursuing her dreams against all odds. It was not an easy task, but patience has led her to be called a pilot and an aircraft engineer.

I decided to write a poem about her, a poem that tells her story.

She is beautiful
She is amazing
She is a role model
Her talents and knowledge struck me
She is a queen
A pilot queen
An engineer queen
She walks in clouds
Excited with the heavy sounds

A young girl she was
Had to stay with grandma and help with chores
Family took off in the wake of her eyes
An airplane took off
She was amazed by the size
She looked up
As she created a dream
With an eye so sharp
Melting on her hands was an ice cream

She did her best at school
Never wanted to end up with a meaningless skull
Whether on a desk or a stone
She believed there's a purpose for her to be born

As God took her overseas
Had to work for school fees
She had nothing in her pockets

As broke as a faulty socket
She never owned a wallet
Just an old model starlet
Two to three figures was her count
Beyond six figures of a dollar was her amount
She struggled day and night
So she can catch up with them flights
She hold on her dream so tight
In the moonlight
So she can walk in the sun that's so bright
Refused to settle for less
And get only compliments of her dress
Working this and that shift
10 15 kg weight lift
Building muscles to defend her dreams
Her future
From the wide awake wondering vultures
She wanted to work across the borders
And carry her documents in folders

After the struggles there is always victory
And the rest remain to be history
Reality steps in
Knock knock knock
Come in
A graduation gown
Shining with the crown
A young girl dream becoming a lady's daily life

From nothing to something that's how she transformed
her life

It was the challenges she embraced
Negative energy she erased
Maintained her dignity
Purity
Brevity
Infinity

She wants to leave a legacy
And inspire the generation of privacy
To live their lives out loud
Education only to make them proud
she who was once a young girl
Matured to a beautiful ambitious pearl
Has become a mother to a young nation
Young world
Not through animation
But turning them to a beautiful birds
So they can rule over the universe

Believe

By: Nancy Lazaro & Kheri Mbiro

1
Mama please don't stop believing
I know dad is gone
And things will never be the same again

No matter how much we try
Look at us, your children
We all look up to you
The strength in us
Is driven from the strength in you
Believe and don't stop believing
We will be at a better place
Let's keep running this race

Mama look at uncle Davis
He lives in the world that's not his own
He curse the day he was born
Cause it is hard living through loan
 And to him every light is a chance to mourn
He has lost hope for a better day
He only need to work hard and believe
In his goals that he wants to achieve
Believe that his life will be in a straight line
All will be fine and his light will shine

Mama, remember when I was of young age
You would let Aunt Bella put me to sleep
As you were busy writing page to page
Of your dissertation so you can raise your badge
You pushed to the edge, to increase your wage
Aunt Bella was always there to help you with me
So you can study and be the engineer you are now
Where is she now?

Mama am asking you, where is she now?
Don't look down
You and I know that she is begging in the streets
While dancing to old and new, ugly beats
She made bad choices
After her last boyfriend dumped her for another woman
She only heard negative voices
But that doesn't stop us helping aunt Bella, our fellow human
Mama, your strength is enough for both of you two
You went through hell and survived, make her believe she
will make it too
Life goes on despite the heartaches and pains
Don't be a loser while life is subject to gains
Mama you can be the light in aunt Bella's life
Let her believe one day she will be somebody's wife
Happily married like she never worried
She only need to believe
She only need to believe

Mama do you remember our neighbour Peter
Yesterday I went with his daughters to see him in prison
We all know he is there for the wrong reason
He don't have a cent to pay a lawyer
Though he is innocent
He can only be saved by a prayer
I heard him telling his kids the other day
No matter what, just believe in you and all will be okay
He still believe there is a day he will be a free man

He still believe there is a day somebody will be found guilty
And he will walk out of the prison door as the sun rises
He will look up and thank God that he believed despite of
all crisis

There is a child who was raped the other street
And on that corner there is a woman whose husband daily
cheat
My best friend's family lives on a meal a day
Her dad is dying with cancer
While her mom struggles to feed a family of seven
Your best friend is a single mother bearing the pains of a
husband who ran away
Your son, Chris, is stressed with poor performance at school
And its been two years our elder brother is looking for a job
Mama, all is left is hope
Hope to believe
Believe in a better day than today
Believe that tomorrow will be way better than yesterday

Look at me mama
My dreams are still far from the reality
But I still believe in me and my ability
With God I will get where I want to be
Just one step at a time, one day I will be free
I look up to you for strength to believe
Remember, through you God made me live
All I am trying to say mama

Is that we are not alone in this mama
Hold my hand, let's be part of team believe
And whatever it is we will surely achieve
Please put aside the negative
That the mind conceive
Dwell in the positive
at the end, the reward you will receive
This is not the time to lose sight
We will make it through the night
Let's fight together until we see the light

2

Yes Nancy, it all boils down to belief,
When you're sick...before pills belief ensures relief...
Without belief.....all is bound to result in grief...
I believe better tomorrow,
I believe belief will deliver me from my sorrows,

If each of us thought along this line,
If we thought of breakfast before we ask "when do we dine"?
If we all believed and look high to almighty and hear his "all is fine"
If we believed together in ours, and forget about yours or mine..
If we believed.....
Tell mama, daddy is in good hands,
Tell her as we remember him, he looks down on us from the heaven stands,

We go forward believing in The Lord, us and friends,
Mama needs your hand as her days she spends,
Dad is gone, and belief in her life on you she depends...
The race is off, and believe me, you're ahead,
Positively, to tomorrow away you have sped...
Mama, the way she has led...
Books, all of you have read...
You're not there yet, but you're better than steady,
You stand out, quite a fine lady,
For tomorrow, just believe.....
Tell uncle Davis a coin has two sides,
Tell him even the ocean has two sets of tides,
Forward still moves, he who makes little strides,
So tell him, "don't despair uncle Davis"
Tell him "you're still in God's plans and service",
Tell him, his life is an unfinished thesis...
Believe in tomorrow n forget the past tenses...
Yes we can shed a tear for aunt Bella,
Or wish to go back and ask of the future from the for-
tune-teller,
She was one of you,one of the good fellas,
Her future seemed quite bright and stellar...
But she lacked belief,
She outweighed her hopes by her fears and grief,
She left the diving board to go jump from the cliff...
But she's still there,
She's still afloat and a thing of the past is the jump scare,
All she has to do is believe and dare...

When you're down, you can't go further but up the stairs,
Give her a hand, and our guts and wits that we can spare...
Deliver her from her misery,
Teach her Belief 101 and close those books of History,
I am
By: Meshack Nyambele
I will tell you what I am and I will tell you what am not,
I am a black man's dream, with my strong fist up high,
I am a visionary, revolutionary, I am a blessing not a curse,
I am alive and living, I am sober not sipping,
A winner when am giving,
A hope to the unfit, Kunta Kinte in roots,
An epitome of truth,
I am a surface to the vine, a stem to my roots,

I am not a shadow or a flag, I am a flag pole, never behind I
stand tall,
I am a dreamer and achiever, a patriot to my culture,
A pride to my father, a blessing from mama's womb,
A light of the moon,
I am poet to a prose, a sound with a fine tune,
I am the change I want to see, I am eloquent, not political
not a just talker in a tux,
I am a big brother, a son and a lover of soul food not the
looks,
I am savant yet a student who never dodged school,

I am not a novice,

I am a voice of the weak, I am not my hair or my skin,

I am who I believe I am, I am a father in the future that's
uncertain,

I am a Scorpio, a footballer, a goal-oriented scholar,

A hood baller, an entrepreneur no white collar,

A hand to lift you up from 6 feet hole,

I am a help for self-help, a conqueror like David to Zion,

I am a leap of faith,

A friend amongst foes,

A heart of a lion, a god fearing man, I am a lord driven soul,

Vision

By: Meshack Nyambele

From Nyerere's socialism, Martin Luther's 'I have a dream', to the
present generation,
I see the faces without a beam, nothing has changed yet
everything has changed and this is my vision. I see the generation
of tight and sag pants, and what's worth is designer clothes,
I see hip hop changing from a movement that inspires knowledge
and expression of the oppressed black and poor community to I
just had heads from 5 hoes,
I see the revolution changing to your revolution which is between
the thighs and its about booty size as stipulated by Sarah Jones,
I see the youth blinded by the heavy darkness of this new demon
called globalization,

What to expect at the end of tunnel?
I see the generation that neglects their true identity and roots just
to fit in this corrupted universe full of mind Brainwash and lack
of truth,
The world of no god and family values, a world of teenagers
talking back to their parents

Disrespecting them just because they've smoked a boost,
So uncouth,
It's a blind truth, no shades just bright light, no sweet flute,
I see a kind heart and the one that's so cruel,
The one that's trying to make the world a better place and the one
that hurls out the godly love,
I see the government that's full of false promises,
And only some irascible riots would move the corrupted leaders
to respond to angered patriots,
Brittle economy with deep sited resources that we possess,
Timorousness of these voices that turned to whispers,
Whispers from sore throats, pretty presumptuous,
Sore throats from screaming for what's taken from us,
I see souls that are tired at these fortuitous opportunities for
having a better life,
Because they now need a more preponderant assurance of their
existence,
I see lack of resilience, no resistance to the interference of the
rights of living,
I got questions, what real happens to the victims of albino
killings?

I see no justice its just us in this league,
We need extraordinary measures and I see none, what allegiance
should I pledge?
I need a vision rather than this, I beg to differ, I need a new
perspective,

Fight, Hope & Choices

By: Kheri Mbiro

As years pass and we burn under a sun that's always up,
We take part in a tournament that we have never won a cup,
We starve in hunger and thirsty, hoping that all is gonna stop,
We boo the righteous ….. and get paid, so for the wrong we clap….

It's a disease,
Hope is deceased,
And fear, hopelessness released,
We break our unity, and quietly embrace our '*hirizi*'….

We allow reason to go, and build hope on chance,
We switch off the music, and hope to go on the dance,
We are all bewitched…spelled to an evil trance,
Living in shadows…waiting for easy gaps that upon we can
prance…

We lost the war to fairness and equality,
We surrendered to hatred and animosity,
We hold the world's record for prejudice and disparity,
And 'Justice'….scarce as it is, now becomes a token of charity…

We wear suits and jewellery, but naked and plain inside,
Evil and vile in our hearts they reside,
We hold on to wickedness as the good we push aside,
We are sick, and instead of Aspirin, we swallow cyanide…

We point fingers, assign blame,
In our heart lingers; huge personal share of shame,
Relations turn sour n ginger, as the picture grows outside the frame,
We all become real life ninjas, in our greedy search for power n fame…

With greed….leaders have turned rulers,
Everyone wanting to be, 'Herr Fuhrer',
We vote for heaters, but they swear in and turn coolers,
The equation balances as the people turn thieves, liars and 'pampulas'.

'I' has become stronger than "we"…..
Our selfishness is open for everyone to see,
'Why limit oneself, if better than everyone I can be??'
'Why own the well, while I can run the whole sea??'

We are infected, we are sick,
The disease is greed, selfishness; and a lot you can pick,
Bugs in ourselves, and less concerning are the lice and tick,
We weaken our wall, as each, to build ours, run with a brick…..

We avoid duties, and depend on a mate to execute,
We shout 'abomination'; while at night embrace that prostitute,
We say we want justice, while the innocent in court we prosecute,
And not devoid of sins ourselves, in streets, others we persecute….

We sleep on our backs, taking it cool,
Who next to beg, becomes the permanent rule,
Instead of the horns, we are holding the tail of the bull,
Taken where he wants, as we haven't the power even to pull…

Yet, we laugh, we 'chill' and relax,
Ignorance hitting the workforce in a record influx,
Education rots, and road to professionalism re-tracks,
'Read'…. 'Write'….what a great achievement in today's marks!!

We lost it….we blew it,
Laziness, diseases, ignorance…stronger in the death pit,
And the fight is on; we are wearing out, staring at defeat,
Confused, paralyzed… 'Where the hell is the last-aid kit'?

But, chewing on Roosevelt's words I always cherish to muse,
"Hope is the last thing, we all should lose",
In this darkness, to stop believing we must refuse,
Getting up to fight, or surrender….we must choose….

The war is on, and to win we can,
Circumstances are tough, but alone we are not then,
Singly we can't…but mightier we become as united men,
Lose the 'mimi-hood'….and build a 'sisi-hood' strong den…

We can….if we change,
Aim we have, let's shoot as the enemy is in range,
To some it's a novel ideology, even strange,
But we deed it before, 61 in Dar and 64 in 'Zenji'..

I'm out of words…but not out of pain,
We are behind, left by the 'future' train,
But blessed we are, of the wealth and resources rain,
We can catch up and gain, if we turn incentive from the fatigue and strain…

We are injured, disheartened….but not yet dead,
The Lord tells us that, 'Our fate is not yet made',
And to greatness, we can choose to go ahead,
If with all the bullshit and blunders, up we are fed…

We know the wrong, so let's choose the right,
We negotiated and begged, so now let's fight,
We found a dead-end on the left, why not try the right??
We know this fruit is rotten. Why keep on trying to munch a bite???

Yes, wake up sister and brother,
The madness of hypocrisy need not go any further,
Shake everyone awake, support we must gather,
Success liberalization is the goal, and unity awareness the mother….

Change we must, and to dependence we must cut the ties,
Less and less…we must feed on 'their' lies,
More and more, they should listen to our cries,
Louder and louder, we should get answers to our 'whys'…

So, the equation centers on everyone's mind,
Choosing to chase the rest of the world, or lag behind,
Keep pace with the rest, or create a new fail-breed of the human kind,
Either way, guilty we all are; as of the failure we all know, and none is blind….
Wake up…..move on,
Stay atop….. Prove failure is gone,
None's a flop…. The war can be won,
Open your mind shop….see?? You are not alone…

Peace & Humanity

By: Daniel Sepetu

Adam & Eve
The inception of human life
10th December 1948
The declaration of Human Rights
And yet humans fight
(Peace & Humanity, Let's Practice What We Preach)

They say; sharing is caring
So a piece for us each
Knowledge is life
Through poet is the way we teach
(Peace & Humanity, Let's Practice What We Preach)

We got brothers in Brigades
Searching peace through grenades
Killing mothers and babies
For a piece of mouldy bread
(Peace & Humanity, Let's Practice What We Preach)
We got brothers who lie
While in the horn people are dying
Wearing suits and pursue an evil eye
While in their homes children are crying
(Peace & Humanity, Let's Practice What We Preach)
We got vampires sucking blood
Pumping their own pockets
And leeches eating our food
Stomping our lovely moments
(Peace & Humanity, Let's Practice What We Preach)
United of the humans will bring humanity
Let's end poverty, ignorance and calamities
Strengthen our friendship
And place poetry to the community
(Peace & Humanity, Let's Practice What We Preach)

Peace & Humanity, Let's Practice What We Preach
It's time to empower women
Give them a right to rule
Give the poets right to spit
And peace shall always prevail
(Peace & Humanity, Let's Practice What We Preach)

Sunshine

By: Daniel Sepetu

As the old man said; 'time heals everything'
And everything change with time so nothing shall remain the same thing
Sometimes you wish you could rewind, so as to rewrite your wrongs
Since the button is hard to find, you live and learn to be strong
Present is a gift, handle it with care
And when the time shifts, allow it to take you there
Be 'fearless' like Taylor Swift, you got nothing to fear
If last wasn't in your favour believe this is your year
To err is human, we have all made mistakes
Human beings got humour; forgive no matter what it takes
You wish you could be a baby, so time could take you back
But you have grown to be a lady, front is where you attack
The earth spins and you'll get to see the sun
The clock ticks just for you the chosen one
Embrace yourself and time will tell
The beauty of life in God we never fail.

After All, They Deserve A Good Life Too

By: Mercy Nguku

Them kids deserve the best too
They wanna go to school, and meet new friends
They wanna learn, play and paint too
They wanna be cared for too

They would have loved to have their parents pack for them a
lunch box for school too
And have their families pick them at school on closing days
Would have loved to be rewarded too
For their achievements at school
They would have loved to go on holidays with their families
And have new stuffs on holiday seasons
Sadly, this isn't the story on their side
They are out on unsafe streets, with empty stomachs
Cold and uncared for
Schooling has become a nightmare.
They live such a cruel life
For them, tomorrow isn't a day they wish to see
Because the sun will scorch again
The stomachs will grumble again
They will be chased on streets again
Because tomorrow is full of mysteries and hardships

Take Nature For A Friend

By: Mercy Nguku

Sitting here trying to understand me
Yeah me!
The sweet me, caring and loving
Me, takes nature for a friend
Me, appreciates the smallest things in life
        A colorful butterfly makes me smile
        Ripples of water makes
        The fresh air makes my bones relax

And the blowing wind makes me want to fly
A male peacock showing off his beauty makes me marvel at God,
above all powers
A glance at a calm sea
Gives me peaceful feelings and heals my heart.
A walk along the sea shore
Takes away all my worries

> I love the birds singing on a tree next to my room every
> morning
> They give me the will to go on
> I know it is God's way of saying
> All is well my child, get up and go face the world

I love the sound of the trees in the forest
The humid air and the dead leaves falling
I love it when it drizzles
The smell of the dusts on a rough road
Whether the sun shines, Cloudy days may be
Windy days too
They all give a meaning to my daily life.
I just love nature in every single way

I Believe

By: Daniel Sepetu

I Believe
That makes me a believer
And I believe like Common; I believe like you
I'm a believer like Lira
Since I was created in God's image-

I see him in me when I look myself in a mirror
I believe in him
I believe in you
So I believe in me.

I believe in day; I believe in night
I believe in dreams
I believe in rain; I believe in Ra, I believe in sun
I believe in pen
And I'm sure it is mightier than a sword
But I do not believe in a gun
because I believe in us and I believe in them.

I believe I'm here for a purpose;
And I believe you are here for a reason
Even when they predicted we'll never pass 25
I still believed in us
I believe in blessings
So let the blessings shower like it's that particular season.

I believe in love; I believe in brotherhood
I believe we can still do something and eradicate the slumps from
my neighborhood
I believe in angels; I believe in karma
So I believe in doing good.

I believe religion was bound to bind us together
I believe in unity

I believe in both gender
I believe in marathon but not the segregation of race
I believe
I believe
I believe because I have faith.
I believe anything happen happens for a reason
So I believe there's a reason why they didn't give Rosa Parks a seat
I believe in I have A dream speech
I believe in Maya Angelou I Still Rise
I believe you will find if you truly seek
I believe
I believe
I believe in truth
And that's what I'll forever speak.

Fight To Win

By: Nancy Lazaro & Vicky Mwakoyo

She was in deep pain
Tears filled her big round eyes
Decision was made in vain
Resulting from the world full of lies
Wishing to tie back the chain
Like cooking food contaminated by flies
Realize your worth and value
Fight to win your daily battles
Her dignity was all shattered
Degrading her woman hood to bits making her mad

There was no way she could keep it thinking of how she would be
'the good gal gone bad'
Realize your worth and value, fight to win your daily battles

She was alone in the dark
No one to notice her swollen face
Heart with a purple mark
Had no clue on clearing her mess
She came out alive only by luck
Her mouth murmuring mourning verse
Realize your worth and value
Fight to win your daily battles

The society expected her to be a 'nun'
That's why she could not keep the baking in her oven
Taking the pill took away her honor and left her with excruciating
pain
Realize your worth and value, fight to win your daily battles

A feeling from head to toe
Of the pain of the lost child
Her self-esteem brought so low
Thoughts crossing making her mad
If only she had said no
And abandoned all the bad
Realize your worth and value
Fight to win your daily battles

The part of the body that was on her for leisure
Now seemed like a curse that she couldn't even measure
Then there she went and got rid of what could have brought her pleasure
Realize your worth and value, fight to win your daily battles

He wonders why her heart is aching
An observer do not know the real drill
Thinking she is just faking
Astonished to see the last will
The moment was passing
Like swallowing a bitter pill
Realize your worth and value
Fight to win your daily battles

It's not right to dwell on the past
So she picked herself up, dusted it off and faced life without spite
Through courage, strength and determination, she moved on and sealed her fate
Realize your worth and value, fight to win your daily battles.

The past is gone for good
Running to catch up with the future
Ants ate on her wood
Now they are out of the picture
She gets rid of the poisonous food
Living for more than just a fracture
Realize your worth and value
Fight to win your daily battles

Never Regret - When Its Done Its Split Milk

By: Kenneth Leon Kolowa

I never regret what I have done
What I do
I just make the best better
And few mends once broken
I know what I want
And that which doesn't intervene with others
I work on my own priorities
Because ask me and I will tell you
I know them better
I stop seeing myself
As my own failure
Of course I make few mends
Because making mistakes is humane
I pray to God
That I do not repeat the same mistakes
Over and over
For how good do we get?
If we moan over the split milk
And grieve over something
That we cannot change?
I will make a harmony
In my own eyes
And happiness will lead me home
I just pray my deeds
Did not ruin your happiness

...Steady...Daddy

By: Vicky Mwakoyo

1

I told you to get out of my sight
You insisted that I was too smart and bright
You are damn right I am, who wants a daft?
Well nobody does, that's why I cant accept this pact

I am a young woman who still needs to study
I want the best for my life and not a sugar daddy
I need a life and hang out with a person I can call buddy
Why do you want to ruin my life and defile my body?

The money, jewellery and lavish clothes
We all like handbags and pretty shoes
Who doesn't need shiny lip glosses and designer perfumes?
We all do though it doesn't compare to my studies

Life's too hard to play around with
To sugar daddies you will be like a bandwidth
There will be no use for you once they are done with
Get serious, pull yourself up, for a better aftermath.

2

You are a sugar daddy
'*eti*' let's go steady
hahahaha... you think you are my daddy
If you didn't know, you look pathetic

Darn boss! I thought I got rid of you
You think I still can't make you
Maybe you are expecting to hear a 'thank you'
Slow your roll dude it is pathetic

It's amazing how life turns around
How with confidence old '*wazees*' come around
With both their two feet steady on the ground
It's weird they don't think it's pathetic

Isn't your daughter my age mate?
Yeah I thought so
I thought that is humiliating enough but in your head you think It's just so-so
Shame on you old man
'*eti damu nzito kuliko maji*'...so?
It is cross generational and that makes you even more pathetic

It's extremely annoying
That I a young lady should be giving you this lecture
Out there and in people's eyes, you are incredibly mature
Hahahaha...it is so funny, because all along you were just an amateur
I can't think of any other word that suits but just to call you pathetic

Street Children

By: Kenneth Leon Kolowa

If every man gives one thread
Street children will have lot of shirts
If parents gave birth to children
They can find they use for them

What about children giving birth to children
What about children killing children
We stand aside and watch
While point fingers to each other

We hold degrees in advocacy and lobbying
Still, isn't it about money we care about?
Companies operate through their human agents
But it is not their children

From the magazine, I read
Dogs let loose to maul children
Security personnel had striped them naked
Burned their dirty but only clothes

They did it all in a real thrill
And seek the applause of men
Men you can name draconic
Who feels the rain, who gets wet?

No child is misbegotten or born accidentally
Some mothers don't know how to bring up children
Some of them know how to turn homes into a hell
Who cares? Of course I do

But only tilt back and stretch out my hand
And grant permission them be my poem
Something is still alarming in my ears
I hear children are social workers

Children prostitutes, children gold diggers
Children parents, children street children
Nobody cares as they lie on the floors
Still it is not their children

When the leaders' bellies never get empty
Is when they strive to get even more
Children don't have places to sleep
Yet we laze about on soft matrices

We have always sought after to be their leaders
They have always wished there was no hunger
You have always desired not to repeat diets
They are children who cannot vote

Jobs are sold, certificates no longer significant
Money beats an intellect of mentality
No word is heard when articulated
Who will attend these difficulties?

Who is perfect, who is not, and who knows?
Astonishing as it seems fall in love
With the word integrity
We all pose to determine the boundaries of

We are evil inside acting integral outside
It start in our homes but it ends not there
It ends in the streets, it is a big problem
Solving it is a problem too but it is ours
Does it take us the guts?
To consider them as our own children?
Or do we live just to face the end of the month
And whatever it brings with it?

Yes I have written to you who say
Heaven made them; streets can find use for them
You cows who were once calves too
Though you never had a chance to be orphans.

The Power Of Me

By: Lusajo Lazaro Mwaisaka

I let my soul drown with the lot
my mind become nothing but my ideas parking spot

I heard them yell
when I tried to be their voice I muttered what the hell

I found myself dreaming of reality
only to wake up and face struggles of my sanity

Should I be the one
should I sit on the sidelines till all is done?

Can I be the change I want to see
can I be a key that will set me free

I dream of how things used to be
and realize that the one thing I can ever be is me

Positive Thinker

By: Miss Mchomvu, Mecktilder

Goliath was a giant of a man. He struck fear in everyone's heart.

One day, a 17-years old shepherd boy came to visit his brothers and asked, "why don't you stand and fight the giant?' The brothers were terrified of Goliath and they replied, "don't you see his too huge to hit?' Then David said, "no, he is not too huge to hit but too huge to miss!" David killed the giant with a slingshot.

Our attitude determines how we look at a set-back; let it be your studies, family matters, basic needs, results in your final exams, name it. To a positive thinker, attitude can be a stepping-stone and to a negative thinker, it can be a stumbling block.

Every problem/challenge comes with an equal or greater opportunity as you can never be tested beyond you capabilities.

Think big and just like David, do not let obstacles bring you down. Just as it is said, "Winners do not do different things; they just do the same things but differently"

I Am A Woman

By: Victoria Mwakoyo

I'm a woman, yes I'm proud
Who says we are weak?
Oh no, they are just being fake
Heavy nine months! Who does that?

Without it, I wouldn't be a complete woman
Who says it's nasty?
Oh no, they are just being petty
It's the epitome of woman beauty

I'm strong, patient and courageous
Who says we are complicated?
Oh no, they are just intimidated
We are the bomb! The name is the impact

I'm important and exclusive
Who says we can be trampled up on?
Oh no, they are thinking before the bus
We are beautiful and precious, that's how its should be!

I Am The Prospect

By: Magulya Meja Kapalata

When you look about the future
I'm all that you can see
I signify how it's going to be
Born to rule and conquer that's what I foresee
First ranked contender I paid the price not for free

Set to face every impede
As the test of what I pursue with no greed
Yes from dark side of the slams with no shelter
I have been in the deep strife crater
Mounting above the stagnant altitude of the latter

Need no excuses but only the past to remember
From the lowest point ever
Now the rebound of conquest is so near
Not yet to be crowned crown but the king/queen is right here
I'm the prospect, through hope the future is so clear.

Once Upon A Time

Once upon a time
My life was in a straight line
Along the way I tasted a lime
That affected everything that was mine
Disturbed the rays of the sun shining
And the moon started whining
About how it's not full all the 52 weeks
I said, stop it and look at my cheeks

Tears are rolling
The devil is calling
And With all these stars
I still have deep seated scars
That bleed not blood in my veins
But of the other and put their lives in vain
Cut my chains, Relax my brain
Put me down but let me rise once again
Cut me loose but am still here waiting for the answer from my last
Amen

Once upon a time
I never knew there was a thing called a crime
Or people can get heart broken
And their happiness can be totally stolen
I thought love and hate are just nouns
Found out they cause too much wounds
Sufferings of the once called innocent heart

That is the essence of the work of art
Yet left my soul with a corrupted mind
And thoughts that are completely blind
Life is a mystery
You got to love the misery
Every sunrise comes with a surprise
Extreme laughter and silent cries
So let life bring on the endless storms

In all its natural forms
And I will dance in the rain
Erasing the tattoos of my pain

The Lights

The night before yesterday, way before the sun came up
I woke up to see three different colours; yellow, red and green
My whole body painted beautifully,
Am sure I must have looked like a Monalisa, A masterpiece, a
perfect work of art.
Then again, something hit my brains, and am all like, red, green
and yellow? Aren't these traffic lights colours?

Stop, get ready, let's go
Red, green, yellow
Simply, you either going, staying or undecided
Doing, staring or dead and forgotten
Sit, stand or walk,
Shut up, scream or simply talk.

It's the red, green and yellow lights
Are you living, dead, or simply existing?
As you get busy insisting on being successful,
Make a positive difference,
To the supra generation,
So they make you their future point of reference.

You must be yellow, with a lot of hello.
Confused if you should say come in or goodbye.
If you should let go or give it one more try.

Most of the time we get stuck in the red light,
or we get pulled over by a traffic,
or we get late because of the jam
but even then life goes on
so Just like we jamming the beat on our stereos, let's remember we
are no longer embryos.

Life is a green light,
you got to fight to survive
as you stick with the right mind.
They say it's not a rehearsal, it's a performance.
A day lost is a life lost.
We live daily not knowing tomorrow has started today,
then we end up with sorrow because of deeds of yesterday,

I live my life,
whether am single or somebody's wife.
Always on the green light,
Red and yellow only perfects my sight.
Cut me loose, shut me down, but you can't take what I have inside,
You can't tie my shoes, you can't take my pride
God is holding my hand, he won't let me slide
To the stars I will shoot,
I will never cease to try

I won't forget my roots or what made me cry
Or hide from my culture, and turn a shilling into a kwacha.

Red, green, yellow,
Stop, get ready, let's go,
Simply, you either going, staying or undecided.
Doing, staring or dead and forgotten,
Red, green, yellow,
Life is a green

The Day Before Yesterday

The day before yesterday
I didn't even have a name
I lived in water
But there was no fish
Only love
Only peace
And I heard they said
I am a blessing
The day before yesterday everything was real
Life was good
Carpe diem is what I knew
My heart was only experienced in pumping blood
And my brain was filled with good memories
The laughter of family
And the friends I made
Without even knowing their names

The day before yesterday
The best thing I did was laugh
As everyone admires the innocence in me
And touches my tiny feet
As they resemble every bit of me with my parents

Time doesn't stand still
The day before yesterday Started fading
Then I heard a beat from inside
It was a traditional music
Getting louder and louder with time
That I started to move my hands Then waist and thighs
Then feet
The whole body was in motion

This music beat had a thing with my heartbeat
Together we danced
Through the sunny days
And when there was thunder and rain
Then the music became too loud to bear
And that was just yesterday
Yesterday
Yesterday
My heart started aching
Ugly moments formed bad memories
I got hurt
I got humiliated

I suffered in the journey that wasn't mine
I looked for treasure
And I found nothing but a bucket overflowing with tears
I hid the secrets deep within my heart
Where my pain were residing
And each passing day
My heart was stumped on
Bruises and wrinkles formed without a warning
My heart grieved
As I dwell in my weakness
Nothing was right

Nothing was wrong Life was vague
And bitterness was better than happiness
Even as it was driving me to madness
I cared less
I thought it's a blessing
But it was a mess
I walked beneath the earth
Allowing my worth to be walked on
I lied to my faith
That all is God's will But it was I
God told me to walk
To keep moving
I chose to stand firm
Like a statue
I chose not to listen to His voice
I chose not to see all the signs He sent

It was me
I made a choice
A choice that led to destruction
It was yesterday
As the sun set
And darkness dwell in the face of the universe

Like Tupac said
"If you can make it through the night, there is a brighter day"
And here is today
The sun is shining
And the sky is clear Ugly days are missing Love has replaced fear
I have found myself in the midst of anger, hate and humiliation
I have found myself in the midst of stress, frustration and
confusion
Walking away from trouble
Before it becomes double
I found the inner strength to live beyond just breathing
To see today as the last day of my life
And choose to be happy
Choose to be free from all the locks and chains

The sky is full of stars
While my body is full of scars
But they are the signs of strength in me
Strength I gained through all the pains
Every yesterday's moment
That brought torment

Is the reason to my victory
A reason for my living with a purpose
A reason for my worth to be lifted higher

And I have decided to walk in the light
Every day, one step forward
I am a brave woman
I am not a coward
I am a human too
And my life is not lived backward
Gone is the old me
I hold on to the lessons of yesterday
But I won't dwell to live another yesterday

The days of settling for less are gone
And those days of believing in others
Before believing in self are gone
The days of looking for excuses in everything are gone
The days of being insecure and walk in the cover of someone else
are gone

Today is a day to live beyond the expectations of yesterday
And the dreams of tomorrow
Today is the day to love more and be happy even more
So when the judgment day comes
My last day on earth
Will be filled with love and happiness

Better Than Yesterday

The past is gone
The future is here
I am not yet home
I walk past my fear
Maybe I am not yet born
This life is mere
A motivation is a yawn
My dreams to stir
I am better than yesterday
Tomorrow is on the way

Shut down the whole universe
Night and day creating my world
Get busy pampering own base
Legacy to leave when am dead
Running harder, my dreams to chase
Honouring creativity in my head
I remember the days I cannot reverse
Bigger than this I was made
I am better than yesterday
Tomorrow is on the way

The sun shines with my heart
Thousands bridges to mend
Though sometimes I get hurt
Got a lot of letters to send
There are doors to shut

Iron to bend
When night and day won't part
Defending where you stand
I am better than yesterday
Tomorrow is on the way

There are borders to cross
There is traffic in space
Between yesterdays and today's loss
Keep running the race
On top of your nose
Rest your case
Pick a rose
With a smiling face
I am better than yesterday
Tomorrow is on the way

Life and Skin

There is a moment of silence in every life
Battles going on just under our skin
Not a minute to enjoy this life
Others ending up wearing animal skin
They want to die and forget about life
Buried alive eating on their skin
There is no meaning left for this life
You cannot judge by the look of my skin
Thinking a lot about life

Sinking in the deepness of their skin
Asking themselves, what is life?
Is it all about breathing and the colour of my skin?
What is wrong with my life?
It doesn't shine even after polishing my skin
Why do they have a sparkle in their life?
While I cannot even taste my skin?
They dwell in the pains of life
Blood dropping from beneath their skin
You will never be right in judging their life
You cannot see their flesh by peeling out their skin

There is a happy moment in every life
That makes you forget the bruises on your skin
The energy that is brought by life
Makes one walk in a bright sun in a naked skin
If there is a dead end to this life
There is a positive voice from inside our skin
Saying there is an opening to another life
Putting an end to the dead skin
Having a thousand reason for smiling at life
Believing there is a purpose for every vein underneath the skin
Always saying, "I am not going to give up on life"
Until I go 6feet under with my skin
It is never about how they live their life

But how do you value your skin
You have to make the best out of your life

Living every day to see a glow on your skin
Meditate on opportunities from the sick ways of life
Departed be the negative voice from under the skin
Rise beyond the boundaries of life
Always remember the evolution of your skin

Tired

I am tired of all these tears
Dripping for the love of ma family and peers
I see a lot walking but have stopped breathing
They know
Maybe they know not
The puzzle that is missing
Mama n papa are praying without ceasing
Too sad they keep wanting more
Embracing pollution permitting it to swallow them whole
They keep turning the pages of life
In the subset they yearn to survive
Busy starting with appendices
Reading the letters upside down
Making lame promises
From sunset to dawn

They are busy acting all grown-ups
Their knives are still blunt not halfway sharp
They are scared of the thunder
Still praying for rain

All night long they wonder
Their lives in vain
Their realness is so fake
Like a burnt cake
That you have just bake

They see the consequences
Then they walk with smelly influences
They hear the mystery
A tale of the smell at ferry
They put their guns down
Their faces frown
Their image known
They seek purity
They forget brevity
They prefer annuity to infinity

I feel like winding up this tragedy
Before it is done
See I will b put into custody
For a man
The cause is ours to erase
It will take more than just hours
But we are better than cactus
Stand up
embrace change to the end of your arm
Never give up
The harvest is too much in the farm

The shining stars are millions
Tears rolling down with every cut onion
We get stuck in every junction
Wondering if we have that many options
The night is still young
Forget about the songs that were sang
The moon is not yet full
The rope is half pulled

Identify yourself from within
Look forward, forget where you have been
Life is too short
Enjoy it while still hot
The beauty of the sky is in you
The life you will remember should be a zoo of its own
You can't progress
If you feed on your stress
And not clearing your mess
Be the shining star
All around
Near and far

This Girl

She watched her father fighting to get what is his
Her mama working night and day so that school she does not miss
She grew up with an appetite for success

Never cared the measures they had of her for madness
With an empty pocket, empty stomach
She saw victory
Telling herself one day all these will be history
Working with people to change and inspire
Her effort will continue even after she retire

Sixteen January eight six the world saw a miracle
Everything happening been a part of an oracle
A family was happy to add another girl
Two sisters to walk together to a well
An angel fell in a family with love beyond measure
Filling every soul with massive pleasure
The sun started to rise in the wake of her eyes
As the sun set she remembers the words of the wise
She realized she is not in the womb of her mother
Time elapsed and she had to take steps farther

Her life was not straight
But she has always known her trait
Every single day was full of surprises
Bad or good, the soul it suffices
Calling it a preparation for a brighter future
Believing it is not everything that need a lecture
Experience equals to the years in her life
Perfecting her ways to be a better wife
Running her race to conquer the world
Proving that it was not a mistake that she was made

Seasons when she was drowning to the bottomlessness of the sea
A bright and successful future is all she could see
When her legs trembled with hunger
She gained her strength in the beauty of a hangar
The path she chose was surely long
Deep within her, she knew her decisions were not wrong
Her dreams were not centred into a diamond piece
Only a heart of love filled with enormous peace
That every life touched may see light
Everyday treating each other right

I See

I can see love in the air
Ready to spread like smoke
I see positive energy in me
Burning, yet to explode
I see people around me
Full of love yet they know not how to give it away
I see people with hands stretched out
Yet they pretend they are cut and crippled
I see people smiling to the sweet lies
They turn against the naked truth
I see people running in the fields
And they don't know their direction

I see people crying and weeping
Have lost hope and pain overwhelm their souls

I see children hurting, living life above their ages
Calling for mom and dad in their sweet silent thoughts
I see women struggling, up and down running
Protecting their babies, loving their men
I see men yearning for true love and respect
Forgetting women need that too
I see the dead crying
Because of the wicked ways we have chosen
I see lovers become friends

The craziest scenario to ever understand
I see changes in the world
I see lives transformed
I see heaven in the universe
I see dreams come true
We have to be motivated
They have to be inspired
All the goals and dreams to be achieved
Before the stories were told
I believed
The life that we were raised
Was a skeleton
Meat has to be filled
The bad us to be kicked
Our behaviors to be piled
The good ones to be sealed
The ugly ones to be jailed

You and I in a mission
You and I taking action
You and I letting go of the fiction
You and I paying attention
It's you and I

The End and The Beginning

Every day we sleep to wake up dreaming
When our minds can't stop screaming
Noises we wish to turn into singing
A song with a beautiful meaning
To go as deep as abstaining
With no abusing
Remembering basic accounting
Getting busy achieving
Where necessary acknowledging
There is no need for acting
We are not advertising
You know we are aging
In this life we are living
It is not worth relaxing
We have to be advancing
Stand up where you are sitting
Better start doing the walking

Life is so amazing
We should start discovering
In and out altering

Without announcing
No annoying
Sleeping to nothing
Waking up to something

So appetizing
and then you are appointing
The efforts approving
Everyday appreciating
People are appraising
The future you are approaching
The past you are assassinating
And they keep doing auditing
You keep authorizing
They are thinking of awarding
You keep on hustling
They are thinking of babysitting
You keep the ball rolling
When they are brainstorming
You are implementing

This Dream I Had

This dream I had
This dream I made
In my head
It has never fade
It is always alive and never dead
This dream I had

Finally it has come to reality
Putting my life in a point of stability
Oooh! This dream knows the meaning of punctuality
Proved itself real at that moment of calamity
When I have exhausted all my ability
Even went to the point of sanity
It was all about my mentality
Turning a problem into an opportunity
Positive feasibility
Forecasting plenty productivity

This dream I had
Leading me to do important changes and leave a mark
Not like a dirty shoe placed in a rack
Or the tires of the trailer of a truck
My combat, I always pack
In boxing I only learn to duck
Even when I am stranded and stuck
I make sure I don't get destroyed by system hack
I will drive to heaven, pull over, park
No one will scare me, not even a shark

This dream I had
Has made me strong over the years
Wiping my endless tears
And my throat peacefully clears
At the sight of amazing pearls
The deaf peacefully hears

The sound of angry bears
Drive away all the fears
Seeing known and unknown peers
Holding a glass up ready for cheers

This dream I had
This dream I made
In my head
It has never fade
It is always alive and never dead

Walk With My Head Up

I was taught to walk with my head up
Confidence in me even when I don't know the map
Every single day struggling to nourish the present
Build the future and make it free of torment
Wake up with a smile everyday
Because I am alive even if I got no pay
I know I have to hustle in every way
One day I might be able to say
So far I ran and now I have crossed the line
In that dark hour, I saw the sign
God with me, told me all will be fine
That I will grow more than a pine
That very moment so broken was my spine
I heard a voice saying it is my time to shine
Below your feet there is a gold mine

Respect To Teachers

To my primary school teachers
Kindergarten, standard one and two teachers
Hands on my chest to salute your work
Respect to the positive difference you make
North and south, east to the west
You are the best of the best
The best among the rest

Without you leading me to light
I wouldn't know how to read and write
Maybe only what is wrong or right
Or the difference between black and white
You made me one of the literates around the world
Making my country proud of the statistics that has gone high
No lie
It's you madam
I remember when I sat in the classroom and you being the tallest
of all
And you were only 5ft2,
You were the oldest too
No wonder you gave us your wisdom

I was too young to understand what is going on
Why should I learn a e I o u?
Or count one two to ten?
Or them a b c d e?
You told me that's the basic
To building a nation that's so epic

Without you how would I know a is for apple
B is for ball while c is for what again?
I know you remember how I used to forget
And you used to pinch me until I remember
And then forget again, please don't pinch me now
I am grown, I read pass a e i o u
I count my money right
I don't let a soul fool me
Because you taught me those numbers
I can read newspapers and understand the world affairs
Because you taught me how to read

I am who I am today
Smart, intelligent
Oh yes I am don't give me that look
Because my primary school teacher helped me
To connect the numbers
The vowels
The consonants
Thus I can read
I can write
I can count
And I can live

Comfortably in the world we live in
Without you
I wouldn't stand here all proud

Bragging about you and how you have made a lot of things able in my world

Teaching me how to write a sentence

Erasing ignorance in my world

You were patient with me, teaching me word to word

I am literate

You still live in me helping me to liberate

Help me God to pass this knowledge to the less fortunate

Made To Conquer The World

You are strong
Stronger than that
So strong you were built
Wipe away your tears
Let go all the fears
You are made to conquer the world
Let your smile never fade
Go out and make a difference
Stop embracing that bed

Shine and rise
Pains are just a way of reminding us
That we are all human
You have the power in you
To look at your situation in a better view
Don't let go of your confidence
It is your personal defence

God made you through his image
He can't disappoint you with no reason
For its Him living in you
He has bigger and better plans for you

Failure is success turned inside out
Use your third eye to open a closed door in your mind
Do not block your blessings by clinging so much to the tears
Yesterday is gone, today is all you have to live for
It's not the end of life
It's the beginning of the long awaited battle
Victory is on our side
Faith will take us places we have never been

Realize now that you are blessed
Live a free life, don't be stressed
God doesn't bless us with smiles alone
Sometimes, pains are part of your blessings package
Learn from the happy days
Learn from the sad days
There is a purpose you are serving
Do not die while you are still living

Thank God for the tears
As much as you thank Him for happiness
He has a reason for it all
Pains are just for a season
Before you know it
All will be gone

Light More Candles

We busy counting money instead of blessings that God been sending our way. Lost souls got no pay, still fighting to smile, yet we wave across the mile then we disappear, leaving their hearts embedded in the sharpness of the spear.

The world has gone to waste, busy satisfying self, embracing those thought to be the best, what happened to for better for worse, if all we do is burying alive the ugly and praising the unnecessary, no wonder we don't last to celebrate a decade anniversary.

Where are the legends we claim to produce? We got artists who seduce the industry as they introduce themselves to the booth or open mic, throw some dices, no luck or good luck, ends up with deuces, then we got to reproduce the lost seeds of our fore fathers.

How many search to reside in the heart of Chief Mkwawa and learn more about passion that it is not fashion but lifestyle, that flows with river Nile, nonstop, spreading hope to the nation that one day we are going to be at the top..

We are only living for tomorrow, what about the day after? We in a death penalty row and we can't even share laughter, the future will be brighter if we lit more candles, and the burdens will be lighter if we shy away from the scandals.

Tempted to Liberate

I am tempted to liberate,

It's never late to escalate

This temptation for liberation that boils beyond the boiling point for generations, lost nations, is the declaration for salvation through education. Yet, not everyone who gets education is educated, but remember, we are building our future here, we need to liberate, know the difference between asking and selling price in exchange rate and how that affects our nation's fate. Let us wake up and stop consuming free hot and cold chocolate, it's a trick, they make us obese, then we can't run no more, we can't run our country to a dinner date just some lunch walks that we always late

I am tempted to liberate,

It's never late to escalate

This temptation for liberation does not seek registration or preparation. It's a self-sensation, personal desperation. Lack of temptation for liberation leads to rough situation and endless brain starvation. I found a station, a location for accommodation of temptation for liberation for an endless duration without hesitation and it's in the population of one and his imagination on the life's balanced equation. This temptation for liberation awakens mind cultivation, remembers the abolition of slave trade, guess the addiction changed the formation to abortion while others cling to adoption; we seriously need affection, manifestation of the unknown suffering.

I am tempted to liberate,

It's never late to escalate

Temptation for liberation has to be put into consideration, for the public to reach safely to their destination with a good reputation that is not subject to lubrication or coloration. Getting a degree has become a fashion, not to mention that people seek attention because of their education. I thought we need to make a difference so one day another generation can make a reference, yet people dream of owning a mansion but they don't want all the tension of facing ups and downs, in different kind of a situations. They can speak about their dreams and get your attention; in the end you will see those are the dreams with passion and not with action. They are full of imagination leaving out creation of the reality out of our dreams to make ours a better nation.

I am tempted to liberate,

It's never late to escalate

Hold your Ground

Some people say why me
Others say life is not fair
Some wish to be dead by now,
While others don't understand why life has to be like this.

But I say,
Every sunrise is a blessing to my nerves.
I might be down and crashed but I serve the one who saves

Problems pile up like books in the shelf
But I am not alone in this; I am not all by myself
I cry in the darkness of the night
Before it's replaced with the morning light
And all my tears turn to a song of praise
As I stand firm, holding on to my faith
I was never promised a silver plate
But God knows I am always on set
Ready for my breakthrough
Pain and success, are like tears and flu
You will be caught up in the corner
But be sure you will come out better than the former
Now hurry up start building your own empire
Before you turn to be your very own vampire

Some people say why me.
Why was I born in Africa? Diseases, corruption, poverty, life is
just not good
The thing is, you didn't take time to flip the coin
And look at the brighter side, the beauty of our motherland
The mountains, rivers, national parks
The minerals, beautiful people, nicest weather
Tell me what we lack
We are the richest continent surrounded by four oceans
What's ours, they come and take
What's theirs, we are struggling to embrace
Denouncing our roots and let our essence fade
We dwell in their lifestyles

Clothes, shoes and hairstyles
They dwell in our minerals
While we banging that track in our stereos
We have constructive option but unknowingly we choose
destruction
And maybe we have forgotten, change starts with you, with me,
with us

We were not brought on earth
To lay on a golden bed
We came out with nothing but a crying face
And they put us upside down as a welcome to the world
Where you will make plans, they will fail yet you got to be wise
To know that you will fall so many times,
Before you have one massive rise

Yes its true, you can be whatever you want to be
Open that door, turn that key
But you got to have eyes to see the rough road ahead
Like Eminem, take the stand, don't be afraid
Life has a daylight
Life has a dark night
Lots of times you will need to stand on your knees
Mostly when you're naked or in a designer jeans
Be content while living with a purpose

Go higher and higher defending your life time status
Some say we can never beat poverty

But I say, hold your grounds
Do the right thing
Remember thoughts are powerful
Think positive

Some people say why me
Others say life is not fair
Some wish to be dead by now
While others don't understand why life has to be like this

But I say
Every sunrise is a blessing to my nerves
I might be down and crashed but I serve the one who saves

Don't Settle for Less

Daily we dream about success,
Plus living a life full of happiness
We want to undress poverty
And caress prosperity
Either through composing and singing a verse
Be it an actor or an actress
Or climbing a corporate ladder
And be on top of the universe
Or being an entrepreneur

And immerse in diverse businesses
Simply following your dreams with no recess
Aspiring to be a prince or princess

Till you get there, won't be easy, it is a process
Patience, determination, love what you do even when it's a mess
The best things come out of the situations that were once worse
Learn from mistakes, live your life, God bless
You are you, not them, so create your own pace
Acknowledge the wonders and thunders with no stress
Be hungry for more, don't settle for less
Daily throw a stone to build your own palace
Do not live your life like a closed case,
You got to fight to win this race
Keep moving forward, the past we cannot reverse
Do not be faithless,
Because even the homeless cast away the darkness, through their blindness
They decide to see beyond morning sickness,
There is no time to impress a soul
Or you will depress a generation
Yet, do not be heartless
Help those who have less
Bring joy to the world, there is so much distress
What you can address, address now
We don't have time in excess
A brighter future's access is not exposed to guesses
Know what you want and live it blameless
At the end of the day
Leave a legacy, don't leave nameless

You Are A Winner

You are a winner
You don't have to wait forever,
Or in a certain weather
To know that you are
You are a winner
A winner at heart
You can choose to lose
You can choose to refuse
You are a winner

Why do you want to give up?
Why do you want to let go?
Winners thoughts are positive
Yes sensitive
Not negative
To make them part of fugitives
They are submissive

That beautiful day you were conceived
Conceived out of love
Thousands of sperms ran
Competing
You came out a winner
Nine months it was
You were ready see the sun shine
You survived
You are here

Thousands end up with their mothers umbilical cords
Thousands join the angels in heaven

You survived
You are here
You are born a winner
You are a winner

You

Your life is not a disaster
you are your own master
Let go of the games faster
It is not easy like growing rasta
And smile to the voice of a pastor

Your personality is so strong
Do not quote me wrong
Just saying the road to go is still long
And your days on earth you just can't prolong
Whether you are in Tz or Hong Kong

It's time now to get out of your cave
There are millions around you to save
You are smart, you are brave
You hold onto love that they do not have
We are in the ocean to face that big wave

Do Your Best

You like art
Thus you are smart
You are tight with books
Like T. Pain with them hooks
You know what you want
And you want it sweet not burnt
Even when you open page after page
Thoughts travel millions miles beyond a normal wage
You know you design yourself to be who you want to be
That's why you keep fighting to see what you believe will be
In your exams, simply come out with the best
It may not be as easy as drinking Crest
Or maybe listening to a tribe called Quest
Hard work pays
Beans don't make maize
Go do your thing
When you are done, you will find my ping
Write good, use your intelligence
Use storage food, surprise ignorance
Go cook your future
And starve the vulture
All the best
Do your best
Come out with the best

Knock Knock

Knock knock knock
It's been a long time since we last spoke
We scream, but rarely talk
All you do to me is poke
Our relationship smells like a rotten egg york

You are such a dangerous specie
Everything about you smells so fishy
You talk of love
While all you know is jealousy and hate
Straight versus curve
Beware you might pass by your soul mate
My life is not yours, yours is not mine
I live like am on tours, don't block my shine
Cried my tears, conquered my fears
Had good and bad days
Be easy and respect my ways

I am not better than you
So shake off that bitterness in you
You are unique and special
Stop comparing the ratios
Think beyond the usual
Dream and believe

You got wings to fly
Yet you want to crawl

No wonder you don't get so high
You are so much attached to the floor
They say, try and fail
But never fail to try
God will make you a head and not tail
He will make you a pie
And you won't have to cry

Walk

I see her, I see love
Near or far, a gift from above
She is beautiful
Inside out
Always thankful
Without a doubt

When I look for inspiration
To build nations
To empower generations
Creating a mind that's ever new
White, so pure, and not coloured blue
I remember you

Every day, 24/7 you are on call
Lifting up angels that fall
Worldwide vision not just in Dar
An amazing human being you are
Shining from east to west
God has surely made you the best

You have everything you need, God
Stand firm, stand strong, Be Bold
Keep walking the talk
Life is not a joke
Lock the useless
Knock into priceless
And walk.

African sisters
Believers and winners

Below The Sky

Sitting just below the sky
Asking myself why
I wish I knew the answer
From within a dancer
Complicated days
Hanging in different ways

Everyday my book of life adds a chapter
Filled with sadness and laughter
Working hard in the field
Praying for a better yield
Through all the battles
I know I am topping up the wealth of my cattle
In my brain
Not in vain

People try harder to bring me down
Hard and good times they frown,
In their hearts
They forget God alone can do that
Lifting me up beyond the enemies eyes
When am so low He makes me wise
I live under his shade
Making him proud of the creation he made
I will walk with my head up
Giving all haters a cup
Filled with love
Their problems to solve

I may have a Cinderella bed
Yet to a king I will wed
Life is a journey
It is not all about money
But positive change in lives
Holding roses instead of knives
The world is ours not to destroy
Only to add smiles and have a beautiful story

Mama, My Superstar

She is a beautiful woman
She conceived me in love
I wonder if she is an angel or human
She is sent from up above

She is the angel of God
Her love so strong
With no code
Even when am wrong

From a minute old
As she hold me in her arms
She treated me like her last piece of gold
No pain no harm
Did she want near me
All she wanted to see
Was a smile in me

She leads me in a way
Where peace lay
Every day we pray
Together we stay
Whether far or near
She is always so dear
With every passing year
She makes it clear
She will love me
Like her last teddy bear
And I smile with a tear
Her love is like a spear
Chasing away every thought of fear
She is my mother
I love her like no other

I wouldn't trade her for another
Not in this life
Nor for a lifetime
Not in a life to come
She is a queen
My everyday next of kin
With her prayers
I always win

I am sorry mama
I know you don't believe in karma
I was a lot of drama
You could have beaten me with a hammer
But you love me more
Taking me higher and higher
Never wanted to be low
You started a fire
And let my soul burn with desire

She is a beautiful mama
A daughter of a farmer
She is a pure Nyakyusa
Bible user
A black goddess
Never left me homeless
She bath me in river Jordan
Inspires me to be like Michael Jordan

She bring heavenly peace
She take life at ease
All she cares is a family bliss
She is a queen
We can't afford to miss
No one can take her place
Or else our lives would be a mess
Together we are running a race
We win by only God's grace
Who can walk in her shoes
A path you cannot choose

Because of me
She had a thousand sleepless nights
How can I be out of sight
She has always been my light
She thought of me
So she was always strong
Teaching me all weather song
For in one world we belong
She love me
All of my being not a quarter
She didn't choose me for her daughter
She is my permanent laughter

She is my superstar
I am who I am because of her
My everyday hero

Refused to be zero
I love you mama.

The Sun

See I am dreaming
That I am winning
As I keep surviving
I am flying
With haters hating
My mama praying
I am moving a level
Making angry the devil
I curse every evil
I know a lot are my rivals
But am up for a revival
God is my survival

Every day I am stepping
Forward I am moving
A better view am seeing
The sun is shining
Bells are ringing
Birds are singing

Elements of Happiness

A genuine smile
A focused mind
A positive attitude
A smiling face

A generous heart
A giving hand
A satisfied thought
A self-controlled behaviour

Believing in yourself
Bringing change to others
Being thankful
Being a peace maker

Be a positive thinker
Be courageous
Be patience
Be yourself

Loving yourself
Loving others
Loving your chores
Living life fully

Frustration

Roads are of different directions,
and at times you got no option,
when your heart is blank with expectations,
and the path is full of negotiation,
that's when you scramble with frustration,
and you are not there during meditation,

everyday there comes a formation,
that leads you to more confusion,
pray that you find a way out of the junction,
that will take you back to your hearts mansion.

Women

Women
We are the queens of all kingdoms
The angels, so beautiful and lively
We bear strength that no one has
Our hearts are full of love and energy
Our days are numbered by the tone in our voices

Women
Look at the tears we let go
We smile for another day
The pains we conquer
Not letting them put us down
The laughter through the darkness
Always amount to our everyday happiness

Women
We are the brightest stars in a dark night
Sunshine in a cold day
We are the comfort of all species
Strength to a man in coma
We shine with every sunrise
A light in the darkest hour

Women
We are that endless love
A joyous smile
Standing tall through storms and thunder
Fighting for what we believe is ours
Knowing we can do anything and everything
We are the Queens and Princesses of the world

Full Moon

Wondering how amazing is the full moon
Where it does hide during noon

I admire it like a tycoon
Desperate for the night not to end too soon

Wondering how amazing is the full moon
Where it does hide during noon

Picturing myself in a honeymoon
Somewhere in a blue lagoon

Wondering how amazing is the full moon
Where it does hide during noon

It is not a fairy tale, it is not a cartoon
Its way better than mills and boons

Wondering how amazing is the full moon
Where it does hide during noon

There is more to life in a cocoon
Not to be compared with a balloon

Wondering how amazing is the full moon
Where it does hide during noon

Not as worse as a picaroon
Where all dissolve in a teaspoon

Wondering how amazing is the full moon
Where it does hide during noon

Win

I didn't know I could win
Even with the love of my twin
I chose what to let in
And I didn't want to be seen

I knew I was a queen
From the time I was a teen
Class teacher, headmaster and the dean
Tears and laughter merged on the chin

In street life I was keen
Knowing the sweetest meat is lean

Depends on how the day has been
Guess you know what I mean

And the desert look so green
But when I observe in between
There are portions that are not so clean
Not wanting them to penetrate the pores on my skin

We Are Friends

We are friends
But we do not blend
We love each other
Like we are from the same mother
Our paths are different
Vision still coherent
We ran miles together
Still, we are not the same weather
We share every moment
Even when it means torment
We laugh in darkness
We smile in sadness
They call it madness

We are friends
But we do not blend
You have your world to explode
I have my world to blossom

We share the laughter
Shutting down the minute after
We are a piece of a metal
Too easy to be fatal
Dead and gone
Found and at home
We count to nine
We see no sign
We think its fine
We cross the line
We are friends
But we do not blend

I Believe

I believe I believe I believe
Yes, I believe in truth
What I believe may not be what you believe
But I still believe,
In God
He created me and you
I believe,
In him I will forever believe

No wonder I live to glorify him
Coz I believe He has got a better plan for my life
I believe
Yes I believe in love

The fairytale love
 The forgotten love
The lost love
That true love
Yes I believe in love
Even with the pains and heartaches it carries
Even with endless tears and sleepless nights
Even with long days and lonely nights
I believe in love

I believe
I do believe
Yes I believe in dreams
And the power of 'I CAN'
The presence of a positive mind
Through the burning sun
And the falling rain
The hustles
I believe in hustles
I believe they always mature to offer you a castle

Tyler Perry made it
Michael Jordan did it too
We are the same just different bodies
So I believe
I believe in dreams
I believe in transition of dreams
Not to nightmares, only towards reality

I believe in us
And I remember that quote A walk of a thousand miles Starts
with a single step

I believe in turning the noises of the world
So that everyone can hear
Necessary noises of change
I believe in the mind that believes
That whatever you believe in
You can achieve
I believe in us
And the fire burning within our souls
Tears running down for generations
I believe in change
I believe in change

I believe in the upcoming generation
The youngsters and the young ones
I believe they can build a stronger nation
If only we do our parts right
I believe in change
Yes
I believe in change

I believe
I believe
I believe

Afrika

I see you look at me in every move I make
You are amazed by the originality
You admire my body, my skin color, my hair texture and all that
the soil has made of me
I look at you and I know you were born in me, still lives in me
A beautiful creation
That amazes this and that nation

You are a masterpiece
Filling hearts with pure bliss
You have allowed my complete evolution
So I can bring positive revolution
I love you with my every sunrise
That makes my bones dance with no price

You speak to me in more than 100 languages
Living in you is 100 percent advantage
Some people think I shouldn't talk of you this way
They don't know for you every night I pray
In faraway places, I will speak of you
And spread the word about you

You are my home, my shelter
We are together, for worse or better
Ooh Africa
Nakupenda Africa
You are my lifelong treasure
The animals, minerals, weather, soil, people is a lifetime pleasure

Till Then

The world is full of frustration
Life becomes sour and bitter
Happiness is found at your own attention
Search for a shade and play your guitar
While wondering about for revelation
Never become nor resemble a quitter
With deep feeling of sensation
Making you a perfect filter
Your heart's full of devotion
Till then, your load will be lighter